Southern Living® Cookbook Library

The Vegetables Cookbook

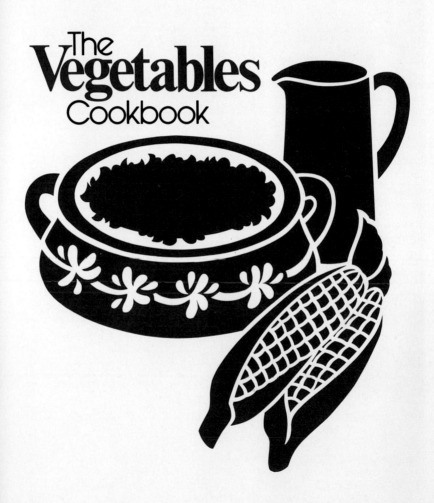

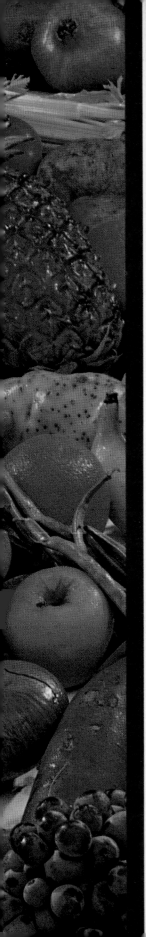

Cover: Garden Vegetable Stew (page 173)

contents

preface

Nature has been warmly hospitable to Southerners. They live in a land blessed with a mild climate, plentiful rainfall, and enough sunshine to ensure two or even three crops annually. Amidst such boon conditions for agriculture, it was only natural that early southern homes included the "garden patch." From these small backyard gardens emerged enough vegetables to keep the family supplied year-round. And southern women skilled in the art of cooking soon transformed this myriad of produce into flavorful, family-pleasing dishes.

Vegetable recipes became highly prized and were carefully passed on from one generation to another. Now, the very best of these home-tested recipes are shared with you in *The Vegetables Cookbook.* Let your family enjoy the best of traditional southern cooking as reflected by these vegetable recipes, created and perfected by homemakers from Maryland to Texas.

This book is even more than a collection of recipes. In these pages, you'll discover nutrition and calorie charts, hints for seasoning vegetables to highlight their naturally good flavors, secrets of just-right preparation, and more. This is a complete vegetable book — and will help you transform vegetables from a "necessary item" in your menu to an exciting course which everyone eagerly anticipates. From our kitchens to yours, welcome to the wonderful world of vegetables — southern style!

Vegetables are a homemaker's best friend. Low in cost and calories, high in nutritional values, vegetables offer the creative cook myriad opportunities to highlight her main course with flavor, color, and texture contrasts. And smart women know that vegetables provide their families with vitamins, minerals, even protein — all of which are essential to proper growth and development and the maintenance of good health.

In this cookbook, vegetables have been broken down into six major categories — leafy, legumes, root, stalk, vegetable-fruits, and specialty vegetables. In addition, the two final chapters feature delicious recipes for mixed vegetables and soups. *Leafy vegetables* are those in which the leaf is the edible portion, such as cabbage, greens, spinach, chard, and the well-known salad greens. *Root vegetables,* in contrast to leaf vegetables, have the root as the edible

handy information

ABOUT VEGETABLES

portion. Important vegetables in this group include beets, carrots, onions, potatoes, turnips, and radishes. *Legumes* include beans and peas. They are characterized by pods (or seeds) of a plant family called leguminous. *Stalk vegetables* are those with an edible stalk or stem — bamboo shoots, cauliflower, broccoli, and celery, for example. *Vegetable-fruits* are actually fruits in the botanical sense but are featured in cooking as vegetables. These include corn, cucumbers, eggplant, okra, pumpkin, squashes, and tomatoes. *Specialty vegetables* are the less common vegetables which do not necessarily fit into one of the five groupings above. Artichokes, Brussels sprouts, mushrooms, and salsify are all considered specialty vegetables in this book.

VEGETABLE VALUES

The whole vegetable family is a rich resource for much-needed nutrients. Most deep yellow and dark green vegetables are dependable, inexpensive sources of vitamins A and C. These two vitamins are critically important for body functioning, but cannot be stored in the body. Eating vegetables daily is one way to ensure that everyone in your family has plenty of these important vitamins in his diet.

The so-called B vitamins are important, too, not just for bodily health but for proper functioning of the nervous system as well. Vegetables are excellent sources of vitamins B_1 and B_2. Dry peas and beans are particularly rich in these important vitamins.

Many vegetables are also high in mineral values, particularly calcium and iron. A detailed chart on page 188 gives the specific nutritional values of many commonly-served vegetables.

SELECTION OF VEGETABLES

Fresh vegetables in season are both a flavor boon and a boost for your food budget. For an exciting shopping adventure, explore the small farmers' markets or roadside stands. Many of them are run by small growers who cannot produce enough to meet the demands of large supermarket chains but who nonetheless take great pride in what they do grow. Search until you find one featuring freshly-picked vegetables which are dry and free of wilting or bruising. Then choose your family's favorite vegetables. The flavor is incomparable!

Wherever you buy your vegetables, look for freshness and crispness. Avoid those with too much moisture — it hastens spoilage. And for the same reason, don't choose vegetables which are bruised or have soft spots.

Canned vegetables provide variety for your menus year-round. The various can sizes offer you quantities sufficient for two or a crowd. An eight-ounce can serves two, sixteen-ounce (number 303) cans serve three to four. Number two cans serve four to five, number two and a half serve six to seven, and number three cans serve eight to twelve.

Canned vegetables are graded according to appearance, *not quality*. Thus, while you may want grade A vegetables for vegetable platters or other recipes where appearance is important, grades B and C are less expensive and just as good for mixed vegetable dishes, casseroles, or in soups and stews.

Frozen vegetables offer another good year-round source for variety. Beware of limp or damp packages of vegetables . . . limpness and dampness are telltale signs that the packages have been defrosted at least once. Both nutrients and flavor are lost when vegetables are allowed to thaw and then are refrozen. Frozen vegetables usually come in packages ranging in size from ten to sixteen ounces. The average package will serve three to four people.

STORING VEGETABLES

Canned, frozen, and dried vegetables present few storage problems. But there is an art to storing fresh vegetables. Green, leafy vegetables wilt quickly and change flavor as the water evaporates from their tissues. Other vegetables — such as corn, beans, and peas — lose sweetness within a short time as the sugar in their tissues begins to convert to starch.

Always sort fresh vegetables before storing them. Discard or use at once any bruised or soft vegetables — above all, don't store them with sound, firm ones. To maintain quality, store vegetables in the refrigerator unless otherwise specified in the chart which follows.

Most fresh vegetables keep well and stay crisp if put into covered containers or plastic bags and refrigerated. Washed vegetables, especially leafy ones, should be thoroughly drained before storing as too much moisture hastens spoilage.

VEGETABLE STORAGE CHART

VEGETABLE (Fresh)	LENGTH OF STORAGE TIME
Asparagus	1 or 2 days
Beans, lima	1 or 2 days — store uncovered, in pods
Beans, snap	3 to 5 days
Beets	1 or 2 weeks — remove tops
Broccoli, Brussels sprouts	1 or 2 days
Cabbage	1 or 2 weeks
Carrots	1 or 2 weeks — remove tops
Cauliflower, celery	3 to 5 days
Corn	1 or 2 days — store unhusked and uncovered
Cucumbers	3 to 5 days
Eggplant	1 or 2 days — store at room temperature (60°F.) If air is dry, keep eggplant in plastic bag to retain moisture.
Greens (spinach, kale, chard, collards, beet, turnip, and mustard greens)	1 or 2 days
Lettuce or other salad greens	1 or 2 days
Mushrooms	1 or 2 days
Okra	3 to 5 days
Onions, green	1 or 2 days
Onions, mature	Several months — store at room temperature (60°F.) in loosely woven container with good air circulation. Onions sprout or decay if temperature or humidity is too high.
Parsnips	1 or 2 weeks
Peas, green	1 or 2 days — store uncovered
Peppers	3 to 5 days
Potatoes	Several months — store in dark, dry place with good ventilation and a temperature of 45° to 50°F.
Radishes	1 or 2 weeks — remove tops
Summer squash	3 to 5 days
Winter squash, hard rind	Several months — store in cool, dry place at about 60°F.
Sweet Potatoes, rutabagas	Several months — store at room temperature (60°F.)
Tomatoes	Several weeks — keep unripe tomatoes at room temperature away from direct sunlight until ripe, then refrigerate, uncovered. Too much sunlight prevents development of even color.

The secret of serving alluring vegetables lies in the method of preparation. Overcooking can produce vegetables which have lost their color, flavor, and texture. Unfortunately, it is all too often such overcooked vegetables which reach the family's dining table — and transform the vegetable course from an eagerly-anticipated one to something which is barely tolerated.

This section was designed especially to help you cook your family just-right vegetables for every occasion. *Fresh vegetables* in season are favorites with just about everyone. When you're serving them, be certain to wield a light touch with the paring knife. By cutting just skin deep, you retain the vitamin and mineral values so important for your family's well-being. And never soak fresh vegetables. Soaking may restore some of the appearance of older vegetables, but it also costs you many of the nutrients which escape into the

cooking methods
FOR VEGETABLES

water. Plan instead on dressing up older, less eye-appealing vegetables with flavorful sauces or seasoned butters.

BOILING

When vegetables are cooked by this method, it's easy to overdo. Try using a very shallow saucepan or skillet the next time you're boiling fresh or frozen vegetables. Spread the vegetables in a single layer and barely cover them with water. About one-half to one inch of salted water is usually enough — allow one-half teaspoon of salt per cup of water.

After a very few minutes of cooking time — about three to five — fork test the vegetables. They should be tender-crisp; that is, they should be soft enough for a fork to penetrate but not so soft that it penetrates without moderate resistance. At this stage, they will hold their shapes best, provide the freshest flavor, and their texture will be neither mushy nor flabby.

When the vegetables you are preparing are tender-crisp, drain them. Reserve the liquid for soups, stews, or sauces — it's a rich source of nutrients. Serve the vegetables quickly — the longer they stand before being served, the more vitamin and mineral values are diminished.

STEAMING

Some *fresh vegetables* are best cooked by steam — asparagus and sweet potatoes, for example. For this method, you need careful timing and a heavy saucepan with a tightly fitting lid. Recipes which specify steaming as the cooking method also specify a small range of time. Test your vegetable at the lower end of the specified range, using the tender-crisp criterion described previously as your standard.

The vegetables to be steamed are placed in a pan with a very small amount of water. The pan is covered, the water is brought to a boil, the heat reduced, and the vegetables are allowed to steam until cooked.

A variation of this method is often used to cook both leafy and frozen vegetables. A couple of tablespoons of butter or high-grade cooking oil are used in place of the water. As the frozen vegetables thaw, the moisture created takes the place of the water and steam is generated. Similarly, leafy vegetables which are cooked in butter or oil exude moisture sufficient to cook them by steam. In both instances, texture and nutrients are preserved by careful cooking methods!

BRAISING

Braising is a variation of boiling. The vegetables are gently poached in water plus bouillon or broth until they are barely tender. They should be crisper when you test them than were the tender-crisp vegetables. You'll finish preparing these vegetables with butter or oil. Drain the partially cooked vegetables. They may then be fried quickly in melted butter or high-grade cooking oil and tossed with your choice of seasonings. (For help in deciding which seasonings to use, consult the chart on pages 12 and 13.) Or, for an interesting – and easy – variation, place the poached vegetables in a single layer in a baking dish, dot with butter, and cover the dish with foil. Bake at about 350 degrees for 12 to 15 minutes – and remember to serve promptly. After a few menus including such delectably-prepared dishes, your most vegetable-resistant diner is certain to convert into a fan!

OVEN COOKING

Another work-saver is oven cooking. Frozen vegetables may be placed in a baking dish with a little butter and seasonings. In 40 to 60 minutes, the vegetables will be cooked. This method is not only easy, it avoids messy defrosting before cooking. Moreover, if you're serving a roast as your main course, oven roasting permits you to cook the vegetables along with the roast.

PRESERVING COLOR

Sometimes, no matter how carefully you have prepared your vegetables, color is lost or distorted. Especially in hard-water areas, white vegetables such as potatoes mysteriously turn yellow – and are subsequently that much less appetizing. Adding a teaspoon of white vinegar or lemon juice to the water in which white vegetables are cooked will prevent this discoloration, even in the hardest-water areas!

Green vegetables may turn olive in color when they are overcooked. Simply be careful to cook them for the minimum time, and you'll avoid such unpleasant colors appearing at your table. Similarly, red vegetables take on a violet or blue hue at times. While overcooking may be one cause of this color change, the minerals in your water have much to do with it, too. A little vinegar or lemon juice prevents the loss of red color.

Yellow — as in turnips or carrots — is a color which is virtually indestructible. Even so, overcooking can cause the color to fade — and can turn your vegetables into tough, flavorless dishes.

DRIED VEGETABLES

Dried vegetables, such as beans and split peas, need soaking in cold water before they can be used. The old-fashioned method is to soak them in cold water to cover overnight. But a modern version of this method saves hours. Cover the dried vegetables with cold water and bring to a boil. Boil them for two minutes, then remove the pan from the stove and cover. Let the boiled vegetables soak for one hour before using them in your recipe.

Some homemakers in hard-water areas encounter problems softening dried vegetables. A very little baking soda — less than half a teaspoon in the water used to soften half a pound of beans or peas — will permit softening without any difficulty.

BOILING CHART FOR FRESH VEGETABLES

Vegetable	Minutes of Cooking Time In Boiling Water	Vegetable	Minutes of Cooking Time In Boiling Water
Asparagus		**Greens**	10-30
spears	10-20	**Kale**	10-15
tips, pieces	5-15		
Beans (lima)	25-30	**Okra**	10-15
Beans (snap)	12-16	**Onions**	15-30
Beets		**Parsnips**	
young, whole	30-45	whole	20-40
older, whole	45-90	quartered	8-15
sliced	15-25	**Peas**	12-16
Broccoli	10-15	**Potatoes**	
Brussels sprouts	15-20	whole, medium	25-40
Cabbage		quartered	20-25
shredded	3-10	diced	10-15
wedges	10-15	**Spinach**	3-10
Carrots		**Squash**	
young, whole	15-20	summer, sliced	8-15
older, whole	20-30	winter, cut-up	15-20
sliced	10-15	**Sweet Potatoes**	30-55
Cauliflower		**Tomatoes (cut-up)**	7-15
separated	8-15	**Turnips**	
whole	15-25	whole	20-30
Celery	15-18	cut-up	10-20
Corn (on the cob)	5-15		

Clever homemakers know that a touch of seasonings — herbs, spices, and flavored butters, for example — adds so much to every kind of vegetable dish. If you are a novice at the fine art of seasoning, begin with the basic herbs and spices: basil, parsley, marjoram, chives, and thyme. Once you have become familiar with their flavors, move on to more exotic ones. Before long, you'll be an experienced and skilled hand at using a pinch of this or that to perk up every dish on your menu!

When using dried herbs and spices, remember that they are concentrated. Thus, 1/4 teaspoon dried seasonings is the equivalent of one teaspoon of freshly crushed. Rubbing herbs and spices between the palms of your hands will help release all their savory goodness.

seasonings guide
FOR VEGETABLES

Vegetable	Suggested Seasonings
Artichokes	Dill, French dressing, lemon butter
Asparagus	Mustard seed, sesame seed, tarragon, lemon butter, nutmeg, dry mustard, caraway seed
Beans (lima)	Savory, tarragon, thyme, marjoram, oregano, sage
Beans (snap)	Basil, dill, marjoram, mint, mustard seed, oregano, savory, tarragon, thyme
Beets	Allspice, bay leaves, caraway seeds, cloves, dill, ginger, mustard seed, savory, thyme, orange, celery seed, nutmeg, vinegar
Broccoli	Seasoned butters, dill, lemon butter, caraway seed, mustard seed, tarragon
Brussels sprouts	Basil, caraway seed, dill, mustard seed, sage, thyme, lemon butter
Cabbage	Caraway seeds, celery seed, dill, mint, mustard seed, nutmeg, savory, tarragon, peppers
Carrots	Allspice, bay leaves, caraway seeds, dill, fennel, ginger, mace, marjoram, mint, nutmeg, thyme, cloves, curry powder, parsley flakes

Vegetable	Suggested Seasonings
Cauliflower	Caraway seed, celery salt, dill, mace, tarragon, seasoned butters, sesame seeds, poppy seeds
Collards	Meat drippings, peppers, onion
Corn	Green pepper, paprika, garlic powder, onion salt
Eggplant	Marjoram, oregano, dill
Okra	Meat drippings
Onions	Caraway seeds, mustard seed, nutmeg, oregano, sage, thyme
Parsnips	Parsley, onion, dill, lemon butter
Peas	Basil, dill, marjoram, mint, oregano, poppy seeds, rosemary, sage, savory
Potatoes	Basil, bay leaves, caraway, celery seed, dill, chives, mustard seed, oregano, poppy seeds, thyme
Spinach	Basil, mace, marjoram, nutmeg, oregano, vinegar
Squash	Allspice, basil, cinnamon, cloves, fennel, ginger, mustard seed, nutmeg, rosemary, garlic
Sweet potatoes	Allspice, cardamom, cinnamon, cloves, nutmeg
Tomatoes	Basil, bay leaves, celery seed, oregano, sage, sesame seed, tarragon, thyme
Turnips and rutabagas	Cloves, ginger, onion, caraway seed

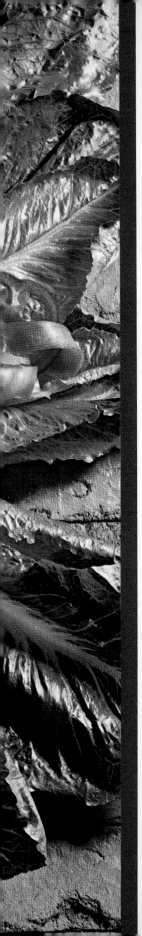

leafy vegetables

What is more appetizing than fresh leafy vegetables? You bring them home from the market, rinse them, and tuck them into plastic bags to crisp in the refrigerator. Your family then enjoys flavorful salads . . . elegant braised vegetables . . . and many other innovative vegetable dishes.

Southern homemakers, who are blessed with an almost year-round abundance of leafy vegetables, have turned their culinary talents toward creating unforgettable dishes featuring these crisp greens. The next time you're searching for an unusual, nutritious, and easy-to-prepare supper dish, try Endive and Eggs. Your family will appreciate the excitement of these two old favorites – in brand-new dress! And if summer evenings leave you too hot for cooking, transform lettuce into the perfect supper dish – Iceberg Lettuce Salad Bowl.

Is lettuce one of your family's favorite vegetables? Then feature Lettuce Stuffed with Corned Beef Hash – a flavorful dish popular in southern homes – and certain to become highly acclaimed in yours, too.

These are just some of the recipes waiting for you in the pages that follow. All home-tested and family-approved – these favorites are sure to make leafy vegetable dishes an important and much-praised part of your family's meals.

15

BAKED CABBAGE

1 lge. cabbage	1 tbsp. vinegar
2 eggs	4 tbsp. heavy cream
1 1/2 tsp. salt	2 tbsp. butter
1/2 tsp. pepper	1 tsp. sugar

Cut the cabbage in quarters and cook, uncovered, in boiling water for 20 minutes. Drain and chop. Beat the eggs until light, then add remaining ingredients. Combine the egg mixture and the cabbage and place in well-buttered baking dish. Bake at 450 degrees for about 15 minutes or until the top is golden brown.

Mrs. Robert Parker, Nashville, Tennessee

COUNTRY-STYLE CABBAGE

1 med. cabbage, shredded	1/2 c. light cream
1/2 c. butter	1/2 tsp. salt

Place the cabbage and butter in a skillet. Cover and cook for 5 to 6 minutes. Add cream and salt and heat for 1 to 2 minutes. 6 servings.

Mildred Crow, Alvarado, Texas

CORNED BEEF AND FRESH CABBAGE

1 3-lb. corned beef brisket	2 sm. cabbages

Place the brisket in a kettle and cover with water. Bring to a boil and reduce heat. Simmer for about 3 hours or until tender. Remove from liquid and place on a platter. Cut the cabbages in wedges and remove most of the core. Cook in the corned beef liquid until tender, then drain. Slice some of the corned beef. Place the cabbage wedges around the corned beef and place sliced corned beef between cabbage wedges. Garnish with parsley.

Corned Beef and Fresh Cabbage (above)

CABBAGE AND DUMPLINGS

1 med. cabbage	1 tbsp. caraway seed
3/4 c. water	3 c. prepared biscuit mix
3/4 c. vinegar	2 eggs
3/4 c. bacon drippings	Milk

Coarsely shred cabbage and combine with water, vinegar, bacon drippings and caraway seed in saucepan and cover. Bring to a boil and boil for 40 minutes. Place biscuit mix in a bowl, adding eggs. Stir until well mixed. Add enough milk to moisten and form into balls. Place balls on top of cabbage and steam for 15 to 20 minutes or until dumplings are firm. 8 servings.

Mrs. C. W. Rowell, Brady, Texas

CABBAGE WITH CARAWAY SAUCE

1 2-lb. cabbage	2 tbsp. flour
Beef stock or water	1 1/2 c. milk
1 tsp. salt	1/8 tsp. pepper
2 tsp. margarine	1 c. grated sharp cheese
1 tsp. caraway seed	

Cut the cabbage in small wedges and remove core. Place enough beef stock in a saucepan to reach 1 inch depth and bring to a boil. Add the cabbage and 1/2 teaspoon salt. Bring to a boil and cook, uncovered, for 5 minutes. Cover and cook for 5 to 10 minutes or until cabbage is tender. Remove cabbage to serving dish. Place the margarine and caraway seed in a saucepan to melt, then blend in flour. Add the milk, stirring constantly and cook until thick. Stir in remaining salt, pepper and cheese. Heat until cheese melts, then spoon over cabbage wedges. 6 servings.

Mary Davidson, Henrietta, North Carolina

STUFFED CABBAGE LEAVES

1 1/2 lb. ground beef	1 tsp. salt
4 tbsp. grated onion	1 tsp. thyme
1/2 c. butter	12 lge. cabbage leaves
1 1/2 c. cooked rice	3 c. canned tomato sauce

Combine the ground beef with onion. Melt butter in saucepan and saute beef mixture until lightly browned. Add the rice, salt and thyme and mix well. Cook cabbage leaves in boiling water for 1 minute, then drain and pat dry. Spoon beef mixture on center of leaves, then fold over and secure with toothpicks. Place in a greased shallow baking dish and cover with tomato sauce. Cover baking dish. Bake at 325 degrees for 45 minutes. 6 servings.

Mrs. Hazel Janson, Pensacola, Florida

DILLSEED RED CABBAGE

1 med. red cabbage	3 tbsp. sugar
5 slices bacon	1 tsp. salt
1/2 c. white vinegar	1 tsp. dillseed

Shred the cabbage and place in a saucepan. Cover with boiling water. Let stand for 5 minutes. Cut bacon into 1/4-inch squares and brown in kettle. Drain cabbage and add to bacon. Add remaining ingredients. Cover and simmer for 3 hours. 6-8 servings.

Arleen Hummel, Shelby, North Carolina

RED CABBAGE AND APPLES

6 slices bacon	Salt and pepper
12 c. shredded red cabbage	3 tart apples, peeled
2 tbsp. brown sugar	1/2 c. vinegar
2 tsp. grated onion	1/2 c. water

Fry the bacon until crisp. Add cabbage and steam, covered, for 5 minutes over low heat. Add the sugar, onion, salt and pepper. Place whole apples on top of cabbage. Pour vinegar and water over cabbage. Cover and steam over low heat until cabbage is tender. 8 servings.

Roxanna G. Pahl, Raleigh, North Carolina

FRIED CABBAGE

1 lge. cabbage	1/4 tsp. pepper
4 to 6 slices salt pork	1 tsp. salt
1/3 pod of hot pepper	

Wash the cabbage, then cut in half and remove center core. Shred. Fry the salt pork until brown. Remove and let grease cool slightly. Add the cabbage, hot pepper, pepper and salt. Cover and cook over low heat until tender, stirring frequently. 6 servings.

Jacksie Fender, Asheville, North Carolina

BOILED CABBAGE

1 lge. cabbage	1 tbsp. salt
5 c. water	1 tsp. sugar
4 slices salt pork	1/2 tsp. soda

Wash the cabbage thoroughly. Cut cabbage in quarters and remove the core. Combine remaining ingredients in a saucepan and bring to a boil. Add the cabbage and boil for 20 minutes or until the cabbage is tender.

Mrs. L. E. Wagstaff, Halifax, Virginia

Double Dutch-Stuffed Cabbage (below)

DOUBLE DUTCH-STUFFED CABBAGE

1 lge. head red cabbage	1/4 c. butter
1/2 lb. ground ham	1/4 c. vinegar
1/2 lb. bulk sausage	2 tbsp. sugar
2 c. herb-seasoned stuffing mix	2 tsp. instant minced onion
1/2 c. raisins	1 tsp. salt
1 c. canned applesauce	1/2 tsp. pepper
1 egg	

Remove 8 to 10 large outer leaves from cabbage, then shred remaining cabbage. Place the leaves in 1 quart boiling water and simmer for 5 minutes to tenderize. Remove from water and drain on paper towels. Combine the ham, sausage, stuffing mix, raisins, applesauce and egg and mix well. Place 1/4 cup dressing on stem end of each cabbage leaf. Fold in 2 sides, then roll and secure with toothpicks. Rinse shredded cabbage in cold water. Melt the butter in a 6-quart Dutch oven or saucepan. Add the cabbage, vinegar, sugar, onion, salt and pepper and toss well. Place cabbage rolls across the top and cover. Simmer for 30 minutes or until the cabbage is tender. Garnish with additional applesauce. 4-6 servings.

CABBAGE STROGANOFF

1 lge. green cabbage	1 tbsp. sugar
1 tsp. salt	1 tbsp. vinegar
2 tbsp. butter	1 c. sour cream

Cut the cabbage in slivers and place in a saucepan with 1 inch water. Add salt and cover tightly. Boil for exactly 5 minutes, then drain. Place in a buttered casserole. Add butter and toss. Add sugar, vinegar and sour cream, then toss until cabbage is coated. Bake, uncovered, at 350 degrees for 20 minutes.

Mrs. W. V. Sirman, Jonesville, Louisiana

Stuffed Cabbage Head (below)

STUFFED CABBAGE HEAD

1 med. head cabbage	1/2 tsp. hot sauce
1 lb. ground beef	2 8-oz. cans tomato sauce
1 tbsp. chopped onion	1/2 tsp. caraway seed
1 tsp. salt	

Trim off outside leaves of the cabbage, then cook in boiling, salted water for about 45 minutes or until almost tender. Remove cabbage from hot water and drain. Reserve 1/4 cup cabbage water. Core the cabbage, making cavity through cabbage head. Blend the beef, onion, salt, 1/4 teaspoon hot sauce and 2 tablespoons tomato sauce and stuff into cabbage. Place in a deep saucepan and pour remaining tomato sauce and reserved cabbage water over cabbage. Sprinkle with caraway seed and add remaining hot sauce. Cover and cook for about 1 hour. Place cabbage on a platter and serve with sauce. 4 servings.

SKILLET SWISS CHARD

1 lb. Swiss chard	1 clove of garlic, minced (opt.)
1 tbsp. butter	Salt and pepper to taste
2 tbsp. olive oil	

Wash the Swiss chard thoroughly, removing coarse ribs from leaves. Shake off as much water as possible. Heat the butter and olive oil in skillet and add the garlic. Add Swiss chard and cover. Cook over high heat until steam appears. Reduce heat and simmer for 5 to 6 minutes or until tender. Season with salt and pepper.

Flora Freeman, Alexandria, Virginia

CHEESY SWISS CHARD

2 lb. Swiss chard	1/2 c. milk
2 tbsp. butter or margarine	1/2 lb. diced process cheese
2 tbsp. flour	1/2 c. bread crumbs
1 tsp. salt	2 tbsp. melted butter

Wash the Swiss chard and cut stalks from leaves. Cut stalks in 1-inch pieces. Place in a large kettle and cover with boiling, salted water. Cover and cook for 5 minutes. Tear the leaves and add to kettle. Cook for about 5 minutes or until tender. Drain thoroughly in a colander, pressing out liquid. Melt the butter in a saucepan and blend in the flour and salt. Add milk and cook, stirring constantly, until mixture comes to a boil. Add the cheese and stir until cheese is melted and blended. Place the chard in a greased 2-quart casserole and stir in sauce. Toss crumbs with melted butter and sprinkle over casserole. Bake in 350-degree oven for about 25 minutes or until bubbly. 6 servings.

Mrs. W. R. Rutgers, Baltimore, Maryland

SWISS CHARD CASSEROLE

2 lb. Swiss chard	1/8 tsp. pepper
1 can cream of chicken soup	1 1/2 c. herb-seasoned croutons
1/2 tsp. salt	3 tbsp. melted butter

Wash the Swiss chard and cut stalks from leaves. Cut stalks in 1-inch pieces. Cook in boiling, salted water in a large kettle for 5 minutes. Tear the leaves and add to kettle. Cook until tender, then drain thoroughly. Stir in the undiluted soup, salt and pepper and place in a greased 2-quart casserole. Toss croutons in butter and sprinkle on chard mixture. Bake in 350-degree oven for 25 minutes. 6 servings.

Andrea Walker, Richmond, Virginia

ENDIVE WITH SAUCE

2 lb. endive	1 c. water
Juice of 1 lemon	2 c. white sauce
1 tsp. salt	3 egg yolks, lightly beaten
6 tbsp. butter	2 tbsp. grated Parmesan cheese

Wash and drain the endive and place in a large saucepan. Add the lemon juice, salt, 3 tablespoons butter and water and bring to a boil. Reduce heat and cover. Simmer for 35 to 40 minutes or until endive is tender. Drain and place in a shallow baking dish. Mix a small amount of the white sauce into the egg yolks. Stir back into the white sauce and heat through, stirring constantly. Add the cheese and 2 tablespoons butter and pour over endive. Drizzle with remaining butter. Broil until brown.

Mrs. Carey Brown, Dallas, Texas

FRESH ENDIVE SALAD

Fresh endive
Sliced fresh tomatoes
Fresh cucumber slices
Fresh Spanish onion rings
Fresh bell pepper rings

Fresh carrot curls
Hard-boiled eggs, sliced
   lengthwise
French or Italian dressing

Cut each bunch of endive in half lengthwise and place one half on each salad plate. Add a slice of tomato, cucumber slices, onion rings, bell pepper rings, carrot curls and egg halves. Garnish with fresh watercress and fresh cherry tomatoes. Serve with French dressing.

Photograph for this recipe on page 14.

ENDIVE AND EGGS

2 lb. endive
Juice of 1 lemon
6 hard-cooked eggs, sliced
Salt and pepper to taste

3 c. white sauce
1/2 c. grated Cheddar cheese
1/2 c. bread crumbs
2 tbsp. butter

Wash the endive and place in a saucepan. Add 1 cup water and lemon juice and simmer for 20 minutes. Drain and place in a greased casserole. Cover with eggs and sprinkle with salt and pepper. Pour the white sauce over eggs and sprinkle with cheese and crumbs. Dot with the butter. Bake at 350 degrees for 30 minutes or until brown and bubbly.

Mrs. Gladden Dawkins, Raleigh, North Carolina

STUFFED ENDIVE

1 head endive
4 tbsp. olive oil
1/4 lb. Italian sweet sausage
1 tbsp. pine nuts
1 tbsp. raisins
3 ripe pitted olives, chopped

2 tbsp. bread crumbs
1 anchovy fillet, chopped
1 tbsp. chopped parsley
1/4 tsp. salt
Pinch of pepper
1/2 c. chicken stock

Remove coarse outer leaves of endive. Wash the endive thoroughly and drain. Heat 1 tablespoon olive oil in a skillet. Add the sausage and stir until lightly browned. Remove from heat. Add the pine nuts, raisins, olives, bread crumbs, anchovy, parsley, salt and pepper and mix well. Press out the leaves from the center of the endive and place stuffing in center. Close leaves over stuffing and tie securely with string. Place in a deep saucepan and add remaining olive oil and stock. Cover and cook over low heat for 30 minutes, turning and adding more stock, if needed, to prevent sticking. Drain and serve immediately.

Mary Jo Bradley, Columbia, South Carolina

COLLARDS

Sliced salt pork or bacon	Salt to taste
1 bunch collards	

Wash the salt pork and place in water to cover in a saucepan. Bring to a boil. Reduce heat and simmer until tender. Wash the collards thoroughly. Remove stems, large veins and imperfect areas. Add collards and salt to pork and water. Cook for about 45 minutes to 1 hour and 30 minutes or until tender.

Mrs. Ruth Mitchell, Tuscaloosa, Alabama

SOUTHERN COLLARDS AND PATTIES

1 lge. bunch fresh collards	1 sm. ham hock or bacon
Salt	1 c. cornmeal
1 tsp. sugar	Hot collard broth
1/4 c. bacon fat	

Wash the collards and tear in small pieces. Place in a saucepan. Add 1 tablespoon salt, sugar, bacon fat, ham hock and enough water to cover. Cook until tender, adding water if needed. Combine and mix cornmeal and 1 teaspoon salt. Add enough hot broth for consistency to shape patties. Shape cornmeal mixture into patties. Drop into boiling collard mixture and cook until done. Yield: 4 servings.

Sandra Methvin, Elmer, Louisiana

SCALLOPED DANDELIONS

2 tbsp. bacon drippings	1 tbsp. vinegar
2 tbsp. flour	2 tsp. sugar
3/4 c. water	1 c. dandelion greens
2 c. milk	1/4 c. minced onion
3/4 tsp. salt	2 hard-boiled eggs, sliced

Combine the drippings and flour in a skillet and cook, stirring, until lightly brown. Add the water, milk, salt, vinegar and sugar. Chop dandelion greens and mix with onion. Add the sauce, but do not cook after adding. Add eggs last. Do not use dandelions with flowers. 6 servings.

Sovilla Anna Yoder, Galena, Maryland

SOUTHERN-STYLE KALE

2 c. cooked kale	3 slices bacon
1 tsp. butter or margarine	3 hard-boiled eggs, quartered
Salt and pepper to taste	Paprika

Season the cooked kale with the butter, salt and pepper. Fry bacon until crisp and pour off fat. Crumble the bacon over kale in a serving bowl. Garnish with the eggs. Sprinkle with paprika. Serve with corn bread. 4 servings.

Mrs. R. C. Hagee, Hiwasse, Arkansas

CHEDDAR KALE CASSEROLE

2 10-oz. packages frozen	1 tsp. salt
chopped kale	1/8 tsp. pepper
1/4 c. butter	4 hard-cooked eggs, chopped
1/4 c. flour	1/2 c. bread crumbs
2 c. milk	2 tbsp. melted butter
1 c. grated Cheddar cheese	

Cook the kale according to package directions, then drain. Melt the butter in a saucepan and blend in flour, then milk. Cook, stirring constantly, until the mixture comes to a boil. Add the cheese, salt and pepper, stirring constantly until cheese is melted. Stir in the hard-cooked eggs and kale. Place in greased 1 1/2-quart casserole. Toss the crumbs with melted butter. Sprinkle on top. Bake at 350 degrees for 30 minutes. 8 servings.

Mrs. Irene Swearingen, Knoxville, Tennessee

DELICIOUS BAKED KALE IN SAUCE

2 1/2 lb. kale	Pepper to taste
1/2 c. grated Gruyere cheese	Nutmeg to taste
1 c. medium white sauce	1/2 c. buttered bread crumbs

Wash the kale and discard any imperfect leaves. Remove the tough veins. Wash the tender leaves several times in warm water. Rinse in cold water and drain well. Place the kale in a large saucepan and add 1 quart boiling, salted water. Cover tightly and boil for 20 minutes or until the kale is tender. Drain and finely chop the cooked kale. Add 1/4 cup cheese to the white sauce and season with pepper and nutmeg. Combine the sauce and kale and place in a buttered baking dish. Combine the bread crumbs and remaining cheese and sprinkle over the kale mixture. Bake at 425 degrees until bubbly.

Mrs. Louise Sweeney, Phoenix, Arizona

KALE AND ONIONS IN SAUCE

1 1/2 lb. kale, cleaned	3 tbsp. flour
2 lb. small white onions	1 1/2 c. milk
1/4 c. shortening	Salt and pepper to taste

Place the kale in a saucepan and add 3 cups boiling salted water. Boil for about 15 minutes or until the kale is tender. Peel the onions and cook in boiling salted water until tender. Drain and combine the vegetables. Melt the shortening in a skillet and blend in the flour. Add the milk and cook, stirring constantly, until the white sauce is thick. Season with salt and pepper. Pour the sauce over the kale and onions and serve hot. The liquid drained from the cooked vegetables may be used for all or part of the milk in the white sauce. 6 servings.

Mrs. Earl Harvey, Baltimore, Maryland

STUFFED LETTUCE HEAD

1 lge. head lettuce	2 tbsp. grated fresh carrot
1 6-oz. package cream cheese	2 tbsp. finely diced fresh tomato
1 tbsp. minced green pepper	1/2 tsp. salt
2 tbsp. minced chives	1/8 tsp. pepper

Remove loose outer lettuce leaves, then remove core and entire heart with a sharp-pointed knife. Blend the cream cheese with vegetables and seasonings and pack tightly in center of lettuce head. Wrap in aluminum foil and chill until ready to serve. Cut head into quarters and serve as a luncheon main dish or supper salad with French dressing. 4 servings.

Mrs. Jerry Barton, Lubbock, Texas

DUTCH LETTUCE

1 head lettuce	1/3 c. vinegar
1/2 c. diced bacon, cooked	1 tbsp. sugar
2 hard-cooked eggs, chopped	1 tsp. salt
2 sm. onions, chopped	Bacon drippings
4 boiled potatoes, mashed	

Remove core from the lettuce and separate leaves. Cover leaves with cold water. Let stand for at least 1 hour, then drain. Alternate layers of lettuce, bacon, eggs, onions and mashed potatoes in a dish. Combine the vinegar, sugar, salt and bacon drippings in a saucepan and heat to boiling point. Pour over layers and serve hot. 8 servings.

Mrs. Ada Borman, Little Rock, Arkansas

SWEET-SOUR LETTUCE

1 lge. head lettuce	2 tbsp. whipping cream
6 slices bacon	1 tbsp. sugar
1/2 c. water	1/4 tsp. salt
1/4 c. cider vinegar	

Tear the lettuce into pieces and refrigerate. Dice the bacon slices. Place in a cold skillet. Cook slowly until crisp and brown. Pour off and reserve fat. Set bacon aside on absorbent paper. Pour 1/4 cup bacon fat into a skillet. Stir in the water, vinegar, cream, sugar and salt. Heat just to boiling point, stirring well. Stir in the bacon pieces and pour vinegar mixture over lettuce and toss lightly to coat thoroughly. 8 servings.

Mrs. Simon L. Bean, Clifton, Texas

Crab Boat Iceberg (below)

CRAB BOAT ICEBERG

1 head western iceberg lettuce	White pepper to taste
1/2 c. butter or margarine	1 can tomato soup
1/3 c. flour	2 c. milk
3/4 tsp. salt	3 c. cooked cubed crab meat
1/2 tsp. tarragon	3 to 4 tbsp. lemon juice
1/2 tsp. chili powder	3 c. hot cooked rice

Core, rinse and drain the lettuce. Chill in plastic crisper or disposable plastic bag. Melt the butter in a saucepan and blend in the flour and seasonings. Mix in the undiluted soup, stirring until smooth, then gradually stir in the milk. Cook, stirring, over medium heat until mixture comes to a boil and is thickened. Add the crab meat and lemon juice and heat through. Spoon rice into a deep serving platter and spoon crab mixture over rice. Cut 3 thick crosswise slices from lettuce and cut each slice into halves. Place 5 half slices, arched sides up, in crab mixture. Serve at once. 5 servings.

LETTUCE STUFFED WITH CORNED BEEF HASH

1 med. head lettuce	Pinch of thyme
1 16-oz. can corned beef hash	Bacon drippings
1/4 c. sauteed onions	Buttered cornflakes

Place the lettuce in a large container. Cover with about 2 quarts water. Bring to a boil and cook, uncovered, until lettuce is barely tender. Drain well and scoop out the inside, leaving a 1 1/2-inch shell. Place the shell in a greased ovenproof dish and keep hot. Break up hash with a fork. Chop the remaining lettuce and combine with the hash, onions, thyme and enough bacon drippings to moisten. Heat the hash mixture and fill lettuce shell. Cover the top with buttered corn-flakes. Bake in a 425-degree oven for about 10 minutes. 4 servings.

Mrs. Margaret Johnson, Jackson, Mississippi

LETTUCE SCRAMBLE

1 head lettuce	2 tbsp. cooking oil
1 tbsp. onion juice	6 eggs
1/4 c. water	1/2 tsp. salt

Cut the lettuce in bite-sized chunks. Place in a large skillet and add onion juice, water and oil. Cover and cook for about 10 minutes. Uncover and add eggs and salt. Cook until egg whites begin to set, then scramble. Place on a platter and garnish with crisp bacon or crisp garlic croutons.

Mrs. Barry Jones, Sebring, Florida

ICEBERG LETTUCE SALAD BOWL

1/2 med. head iceberg lettuce	1/2 c. thinly sliced celery
1 sm. red apple	1/2 c. French dressing
1/2 sm. Bermuda onion	

Shred the lettuce. Cut the apple in half and remove the core. Cut in thin slices. Peel and thinly slice onion. Combine the lettuce, apple, onion and celery in a large salad bowl. Drizzle dressing over top and toss lightly. 6 servings.

Mrs. Hoyt Williams, Purcell, Oklahoma

WILTED LETTUCE SALAD

Leaf lettuce, cleaned and chopped	1/2 c. vinegar
4 green onions, diced	1 tbsp. sugar
3 hard-cooked eggs, diced	Garlic salt to taste
1/2 lb. bacon	

Mix the lettuce, onions and eggs. Fry the bacon until crisp and remove from pan. Crumble. Add the vinegar, sugar and garlic salt to bacon drippings and heat to boiling point. Pour over the lettuce mixture and toss until lettuce is coated. Add the bacon and serve immediately. 6 servings.

Mrs. David Hays, Flemington, West Virginia

TOSSED SALAD

1 clove of garlic	1/2 c. salad oil
1 hard-cooked egg	2 tbsp. chopped parsley
1/4 tsp. dry mustard	1/2 lb. spinach
1/4 tsp. pepper	1 onion, thinly sliced
1/2 tsp. salt	1/2 head lettuce
1/4 c. vinegar	

Rub a large bowl with cut garlic clove. Place the egg yolk in the bowl and mash with a wooden spoon. Blend the mustard, pepper, salt, vinegar, oil and parsley with egg yolk. Tear spinach into small pieces. Add onion, spinach and chopped egg white to dressing. Break the lettuce into bite-sized pieces and add to salad mixture. Toss lightly. 6 servings.

Ruth G. Erickson, Frankfort, Kentucky

CAESAR SALAD

5/8 c. salad oil	1/4 c. crumbled bleu cheese
1 clove of garlic, minced	1/4 c. lemon juice
2 c. bread cubes	1/4 tsp. hot sauce
1 lge. head romaine	3/4 tsp. salt
1 lge. head lettuce	1/4 tsp. dry mustard
1/4 c. Parmesan cheese	1 egg

Heat 2 tablespoons salad oil in a skillet and add the garlic and bread cubes. Heat until light brown, then remove from heat. Tear romaine and lettuce into bite-sized pieces and place in a salad bowl. Sprinkle the lettuce with cheeses. Combine remaining salad oil, lemon juice, hot sauce, salt and dry mustard in a jar. Cover and shake. Pour dressing over salad greens and toss lightly. Break the egg into greens and mix until egg particles disappear. Add croutons and toss. 6 servings.

Catherine Penton, Lubbock, Texas

SCALLOPED SPINACH

1 tbsp. minced onion	1/2 tsp. salt
2 eggs, well beaten	1/4 tsp. pepper
2/3 c. milk	1 1-lb. can spinach, drained
1/3 c. grated cheese	1/2 c. buttered bread crumbs

Mix the onion, eggs, milk, cheese, salt and pepper in a casserole. Add the spinach and mix thoroughly. Top with bread crumbs. Bake in 350-degree oven for 30 minutes. 4 servings.

Mrs. Nancy Carter, Fayetteville, Arkansas

MUSHROOM-SPINACH SUPREME

1 lb. fresh mushrooms	1/4 c. sliced almonds
Butter or margarine	1 can cream of mushroom soup
2 pkg. frozen spinach	Garlic salt to taste
1 tbsp. sesame seed	1 c. grated Cheddar cheese

Wash and drain the mushrooms. Cut off stems. Saute the mushroom stems and caps in a small amount of butter in a saucepan until brown. Cook the spinach according to package directions and drain thoroughly. Saute sesame seed and almonds in small amount of butter until brown. Combine the mushroom soup, sesame seed, almonds and garlic salt and add spinach. Pour into a 1-quart casserole. Top with mushrooms and cover with cheese. Bake at 325 degrees for 1 hour or until cheese is melted and browned. 6-8 servings.

Agnes Dervishian, Fort Worth, Texas

CREAMED SPINACH HUNGARIAN

1 pkg. frozen chopped spinach	1 c. hot cream
1 med. onion, finely chopped	Salt and pepper to taste
3 tbsp. melted butter	1/4 tsp. nutmeg
2 1/2 tbsp. flour	

Cook the spinach according to package directions and drain. Saute the onion in butter in a saucepan for 3 minutes. Blend in the flour. Add cream gradually and cook until thick, stirring constantly. Add the spinach and season with salt and pepper. Add nutmeg and mix well. 4 servings.

Doris S. Hills, Elizabeth, Louisiana

PINEAPPLE-GREEN RICE CASSEROLE

1 c. rice	1 c. evaporated milk
2 tsp. salt	1/4 c. melted butter
1 1/2 c. water	1 c. grated sharp Cheddar
1 9-oz. package frozen	cheese
spinach	1 tbsp. minced onion
1 13 1/2-oz. can pineapple	1/3 c. finely chopped parsley
tidbits, well drained	1 tsp. Worcestershire sauce
2 eggs, beaten	

Combine the rice, salt and water in a saucepan and heat to boiling point. Cover and reduce heat. Simmer for 15 minutes. Cook the spinach according to package directions and drain well. Mix in the rice and remaining ingredients and turn into a greased casserole. Bake in a 350-degree oven for 40 to 45 minutes. 6 servings.

Mrs. P. G. Arnold, Chapel Hill, North Carolina

BAKED SPINACH WITH CREAMED VEGETABLE SAUCE

2 10-oz. packages frozen chopped
   spinach
1/2 c. bread crumbs
1/2 tsp. salt
1/8 tsp. pepper

1/2 c. milk
2 eggs, beaten
3/4 c. slivered almonds
1/3 c. melted butter

Cook the spinach according to package directions, then drain. Blend all ingredients and pack into a buttered 1-quart casserole. Bake at 325 degrees for 45 minutes to 1 hour or until set. Unmold on a platter.

Creamed Vegetable Sauce

1/4 c. butter
1/3 c. diced onion
1/4 c. flour
2 c. milk

1/2 c. diced cooked carrots
1/2 c. cooked peas
1/2 c. diced cooked celery

Melt the butter in a saucepan. Add the onion and cook until soft but not brown. Blend in the flour. Add the milk gradually, stirring constantly, and cook and stir until smooth and thickened. Add remaining ingredients and heat thoroughly. Pour over spinach mixture. Garnish with carrot slices and parsley, if desired. 6-8 servings.

SPINACH BALLS

2 c. drained cooked spinach
2 tbsp. butter

1/2 to 1 tsp. salt
1/4 tsp. pepper

2 eggs	1/8 tsp. allspice
Bread crumbs	1/4 tsp. oregano
2 tbsp. grated onion	1/4 c. water
2 tbsp. grated cheese	

Combine the spinach, butter, salt, pepper, 1 egg, 1 cup bread crumbs, onion, cheese and spices in a bowl and let stand for 10 minutes. Shape into balls. Blend remaining egg and water. Roll spinach balls in bread crumbs, then in egg mixture. Roll again in crumbs. Fry in deep fat at 375 degrees until brown. Drain on absorbent paper. 6 servings.

Mrs. Reva Bishop, Vine Grove, Kentucky

SERBIAN SPINACH

1 carton cottage cheese	1/4 c. melted margarine
3 tbsp. flour	1/4 lb. sharp cheese, grated
3 eggs, lightly beaten	1 pkg. frozen chopped spinach

Mix the cottage cheese, flour, eggs, margarine and grated cheese in a casserole. Cook the spinach according to package directions and drain. Add to egg mixture and mix well. Bake at 350 degrees for 1 hour. 6 servings.

Mrs. Ruth Marie Skaggs, Morgantown, West Virginia

SPINACH LOAF

3 tbsp. melted butter	1/2 c. mayonnaise
3 tbsp. flour	Salt and pepper to taste
1 No. 2 can spinach	3 eggs, well beaten
1 c. milk	

Blend the butter and flour in a saucepan. Drain the spinach and reserve 1/2 cup liquid. Add reserved liquid to flour mixture, then stir in the milk. Cook, stirring, until thickened. Remove from heat. Chop the spinach and add to sauce. Stir in the mayonnaise, salt, pepper and eggs. Pour into a buttered casserole and set casserole in shallow pan of water. Bake at 400 degrees for about 45 minutes or until brown.

Mrs. H. C. Peterson, Austin, Texas

SPINACH WITH GRAPEFRUIT SECTIONS

3 lb. fresh spinach	Salt and pepper to taste
1 No. 2 can grapefruit sections, drained	Butter to taste

Wash the spinach and place in a saucepan. Cover and cook for 7 to 8 minutes. Drain and chop. Warm the grapefruit sections and fold into spinach. Season with salt, pepper and butter. 6 servings.

Mrs. Lillian P. Dunbar, Greensboro, North Carolina

SPINACH MADELEINE

2 pkg. frozen chopped spinach	3/4 tsp. celery salt
4 tbsp. butter	3/4 tsp. garlic salt
2 tbsp. flour	1/2 tsp. salt
2 tbsp. chopped onion	1 tsp. Worcestershire sauce
1/2 c. evaporated milk	1 6-oz. roll jalapeno
1/2 tsp. pepper	cheese
Red pepper to taste	Buttered bread crumbs

Cook the spinach according to package directions. Drain and reserve 1/2 cup liquid. Melt the butter in a saucepan. Add the flour and stir until blended. Add onion and cook until soft. Add the milk and reserved spinach liquid slowly and cook, stirring, until smooth and thick. Add seasonings and Worcestershire sauce. Cut the cheese in small pieces and add to sauce. Cook, stirring, until cheese is melted, then stir in spinach. Place in a casserole and cover with buttered crumbs. Bake at 350 degrees for 25 minutes.

Mrs. Ethel Robbins, Jennings, Louisiana

SPINACH PIE

1/2 c. shortening	4 c. milk
2 1/2 c. flour	1 1/4 tsp. salt
4 c. chopped fresh spinach	1/2 c. chopped bacon
4 eggs, well beaten	

Cut the shortening into the flour in a bowl and stir in just enough cold water to moisten flour. Roll out on a floured board and place in a square baking dish. Place the spinach in pastry. Combine the eggs, milk and salt in a bowl and mix well. Pour over spinach and top with bacon. Bake at 450 degrees for 10 minutes. Reduce temperature to 350 degrees and bake until set. Egg white may be brushed over pastry before adding filling to prevent sogginess. 6 servings.

Janice Bendshadler, Tempe, Arizona

SPINACH TIMBALES

4 slices bacon, diced	2 tbsp. butter or margarine
1 No. 2 1/2 can spinach, drained	2 tbsp. flour
3 eggs, slightly beaten	1/2 c. cold milk
Salt and pepper to taste	1/2 c. hot milk

Fry the bacon in a frypan until crisp and add bacon and drippings to spinach in a bowl. Add eggs and seasonings and mix well. Fill greased custard cups 2/3 full with spinach mixture. Bake at 350 degrees for 40 minutes. Melt the butter in a double boiler and blend in flour. Add cold milk and blend well. Stir in the hot milk and cook, stirring, until smooth and thick. Add salt and pepper and cover. Cook for 5 to 8 minutes. Unmold spinach and serve with sauce. 6 servings.

June Houchins, Coleman, Texas

Spanish-Style Eggs and Spinach (below)

SPANISH-STYLE EGGS AND SPINACH

1 10-oz. package frozen chopped spinach	4 peppercorns
3/4 c. sliced pimento-stuffed olives	Dash of ground cumin
	2 slices bread
20 almonds	3 tbsp. olive or salad oil
1 clove of garlic	2/3 c. beef or chicken bouillon
1 whole clove	4 eggs
	1 1/2 tbsp. melted butter

Cook the spinach according to package directions but without salt, then drain. Combine 1/2 cup olives, almonds, garlic, clove, peppercorns and cumin in an electric blender and blend until finely chopped. Crumble the bread and fry in hot oil until browned. Add to blender. Add the bouillon and blend thoroughly. Toss with spinach and spoon into 4 greased individual baking dishes. Break an egg into the center of spinach in each dish and spoon part of the butter over each egg. Bake in 350-degree oven for 15 minutes or until egg yolks are set. Garnish with remaining olive slices. 4 servings.

HERBED SPINACH BAKE

1 pkg. frozen chopped spinach	1/3 c. milk
1 c. brown rice	2 tsp. chopped onion
1 c. grated American cheese	1/2 tsp. Worcestershire sauce
2 eggs, slightly beaten	1/4 tsp. rosemary
2 tbsp. melted margarine	1 tsp. salt

Cook the spinach and brown rice according to package directions. Combine the spinach, rice and remaining ingredients and pour into a casserole. Bake at 350 degrees for 20 to 25 minutes. 8 servings.

Mrs. F. M. Woodson, Alva, Oklahoma

Spinach Ring (below)

SPINACH RING

2 10-oz. packages frozen leaf spinach	2 eggs, slightly beaten
1/4 c. melted butter	1 1/2 tsp. minced onion
	Dash of pepper

Cook the spinach according to package directions, then drain. Add remaining ingredients and mix thoroughly. Spoon into a well-greased 3-cup ring mold and place in a pan of hot water. Bake at 375 degrees for 30 minutes or until firm. Unmold. Fill center with creamed hard-cooked eggs and top with cooked, crumbled bacon, if desired. 4-5 servings.

RICE AND SPINACH

1 sm. potato, cut in cubes	1 lge. can spinach, drained
2 tbsp. rice	Salt and pepper to taste
2 slices bacon, diced	1 tbsp. vinegar
1 1/2 c. water	

Combine the potato, rice, bacon and water in a saucepan and bring to a boil. Reduce heat and simmer until rice and potato are done. Add the spinach, salt, pepper and vinegar and heat through.

Mrs. Elizabeth Vornsand, Weimar, Texas

SPINACH WITH BACON

1 1/2 lb. fresh spinach	Salt to taste
5 slices bacon	3 hard-cooked eggs, sliced

Wash the spinach thoroughly and place in a saucepan in water to cover. Bring to a boil and reduce heat. Simmer until done. Drain. Cook the bacon in a skillet until crisp. Remove from skillet and cool. Crumble the bacon and add to spinach. Add desired amount of bacon drippings for seasoning. Add salt and place in a serving dish. Garnish with eggs.

Ethel Watkins, Pendleton, South Carolina

SPRING TURNIP GREENS

2 lb. turnip greens	1/2 c. bacon drippings
2 c. water	Salt to taste

Wash the turnip greens well and place in a kettle with the water. Cook for about 30 minutes or until greens are tender. Drain and chop fine. Add bacon drippings and salt and cook, stirring, until heated through. 6 servings.

Mrs. Elbert Taylor, Carthage, North Carolina

SESAME-CHEESE GREENS

2 c. cooked turnip greens, seasoned	1/4 lb. cheese, grated
	1 tbsp. toasted sesame seed

Place the turnip greens on a platter and sprinkle with cheese and sesame seed.

Mildred Fowler, Woodruff, South Carolina

TURNIP GREENS WITH CORNMEAL DUMPLINGS

2 bunches turnip greens	1/4 tsp. pepper
Bacon drippings to taste	1/2 tsp. celery seed
2 c. cornmeal	1/2 c. finely chopped onion
1/2 tsp. sugar	2 tbsp. melted shortening
1 tsp. salt	

Wash the turnip greens and place in a saucepan. Add bacon drippings and 1/2 cup water and bring to a boil. Cover and reduce heat. Simmer for 20 minutes. Sift the cornmeal, sugar, salt and pepper into a bowl. Stir in the celery seed, onion and enough boiling water to make a stiff dough. Add the shortening and cover. Let stand for 4 to 5 minutes. Shape into small balls and drop on top of turnip greens. Cook for 20 to 30 minutes. 6-8 servings.

Mrs. W. S. Solomon, Atmore, Alabama

Combination Bean Salad (page 38)

legumes

Lima beans, black-eyed peas, soybeans, green peas, green beans, pinto beans, and more — all are legumes. These nutrition-packed vegetables are available almost year-round and are among the best sources of protein, vitamins, and minerals in the entire vegetable family. Many legumes grow well in the Southland — and southern homemakers have for years featured them at their tables.

From their recipes, the very finest are now shared with you. Discover what Southerners call "butter beans" — maybe you know them better as limas! Whether you serve Gourmet Limas and Mushrooms or Butter Beans in Savory Sauce, you're certain to draw compliments from your family! There are few dishes more completely southern than Black-eyed Peas and Fresh Okra. Introduce your family to this long-time favorite in Dixie with the recipe you'll find in this section. And from the far western corner of the South comes Frijoles — pinto beans which are cooked, mashed, and fried. Originally a Mexican dish, it was shared with Texans who then passed it on to their fellow Southerners.

On extra-special occasions when you want vegetable dishes that make people sit up and take notice, serve Amandine Peas and Onions or Dilled Green Beans. Both recipes feature a blend of vegetables and seasonings which will make them party-perfect dishes. Why not explore the excitement of legumes, now, in the recipe-rich pages which follow!

COMBINATION BEAN SALAD

1 9-oz. package frozen French green beans with toasted almonds	1/4 c. vinegar
	2 tbsp. sugar
	1/4 tsp. dry mustard
1 10-oz. package frozen corn and peas with tomatoes	Lettuce leaves
	1 15-oz. can red kidney beans, drained
4 tbsp. salad oil	

Prepare the frozen vegetables separately according to package directions, reserving the bag of almonds from the green beans and substituting 1 tablespoon salad oil for the butter in cooking each vegetable. Do not drain. Cool. Combine remaining salad oil with vinegar, sugar and mustard and stir until blended. Line a salad bowl with lettuce. Arrange green beans, corn and kidney beans in 3 separate sections in bowl. Chill. Sprinkle salad oil mixture over salad just before serving, then sprinkle with reserved almonds. About 8 servings.

Photograph for this recipe on page 36.

LOUISIANA LIMA BEANS

1/2 lb. small pork sausage links	2 tbsp. chopped onion
2 c. cooked dried lima beans	2 tbsp. shredded green pepper
1 tsp. salt	2 tbsp. butter
1/4 tsp. poultry seasoning	1 c. milk
Pepper to taste	

Parboil the sausage in a small amount of water for 5 minutes. Combine the beans and seasonings in a buttered casserole and add the sausage. Sprinkle with the onion and green pepper and dot with butter. Cover with milk. Bake at 350 degrees for 25 minutes. 4 servings.

Mrs. Jo Frances Weimar, Alto, Texas

LIMA BEAN-OLIVE CASSEROLE

1 c. chopped onions	1 clove of garlic, minced
1 c. chopped green peppers	1 tsp. salt
4 tbsp. olive oil or bacon drippings	1 tbsp. cornstarch
	3 cans baby green lima beans
1 c. chopped ripe olives	1 c. grated Cheddar cheese
1 tbsp. chili powder	

Preheat oven to 375 degrees. Saute the onions and green peppers in oil in a skillet until tender. Combine the olives, chili powder, garlic, salt and cornstarch in a saucepan. Drain the lima beans and reserve 1 1/4 cups liquid. Stir reserved liquid into cornstarch mixture and cook until slightly thickened. Add onion mixture, beans and half the cheese and place in a greased casserole. Bake for 30 minutes. Sprinkle with remaining cheese and bake until cheese is melted. May be prepared day before serving and refrigerated or frozen. 18-20 servings.

Mrs. Ivanell S. Harris, Florence, Mississippi

BAKED LIMA BEANS WITH TOMATO SAUCE

1 1/2 c. dried lima beans	1 clove of garlic, minced
5 c. cold water	2 tbsp. flour
4 slices bacon	1 1/2 c. canned tomatoes
1/3 c. minced celery	2 tsp. salt
1/2 c. minced onion	1/8 tsp. pepper
1/4 c. diced green pepper	2 tbsp. sugar

Wash the beans and soak overnight in 3 cups cold water. Add the remaining water and cover. Bring to a boil. Simmer for 30 minutes or until tender, then drain. Place in a 1 1/2-quart casserole. Cut bacon in 1-inch pieces and fry in skillet until crisp. Add the celery, onion, green pepper and garlic. Cook until the vegetables are tender. Stir in the flour, tomatoes, salt, pepper and sugar. Cook until thickened, stirring constantly. Pour the sauce over the beans. Bake, covered, at 300 degrees for 1 hour. 4 servings.

Mrs. Michael Elwood, Flagstaff, Arizona

LIMA BEAN-SAUSAGE BAKE

2 c. dried lima beans	1 c. catsup
6 c. water	1 tsp. horseradish
2 tsp. salt	2 tsp. Worcestershire sauce
2 lb. pork sausage links	2 tbsp. brown sugar
1/2 c. chopped onion	

Wash the lima beans and cover with the water. Bring to a boil and boil for 2 minutes. Remove from heat and let stand, covered, for 1 hour. Add the salt and simmer for about 1 hour or until tender. Drain, reserving the liquid. Brown the sausage links in skillet, then remove from skillet. Add the onion and cook until soft. Remove from skillet and add to the beans. Combine the catsup, 1/4 cup reserved liquid, horseradish, Worcestershire sauce and brown sugar and add to the bean mixture. Place half the beans in a greased 2 1/2-quart casserole. Top with half the sausage. Repeat layers. Bake at 350 degrees for 35 to 40 minutes. 8 servings.

Mrs. Maude Swift, Charlotte, North Carolina

LIMA BEANS DELUXE

3 1/2 c. cooked fresh lima beans	1 1/3 c. hot light cream
3 tbsp. butter, melted	2 egg yolks, well beaten
1 tsp. sugar	1/4 tsp. salt
1 tbsp. minced parsley	Paprika

Combine the lima beans, butter, sugar and parsley in a saucepan and bring to a boil over low heat. Place the beans in a serving dish. Stir the cream into the egg yolks and add the salt. Cook over low heat for 1 to 2 minutes and do not boil. Pour the sauce over the beans and sprinkle with paprika. 6-8 servings.

Mrs. Print Huff, Byrdstown, Tennessee

Lima Bean Bake (below)

LIMA BEAN BAKE

4 c. dried lima beans	1/2 tsp. hot sauce
3 tsp. salt	1 tsp. dry mustard
1/2 c. unsulphured molasses	2 med. onions, sliced
1/2 c. chili sauce	2 c. diced cooked ham or
2 tbsp. vinegar	luncheon meat

Wash the lima beans and place in a deep kettle. Add the salt and 2 quarts boiling water and cover. Simmer for 2 hours or until tender, adding more water, if necessary. Drain the beans and reserve 1 cup liquid. Combine the molasses, chili sauce, vinegar, hot sauce, mustard and reserved lima bean liquid and mix well. Layer the beans, onions and ham in a 3-quart casserole and pour molasses mixture over beans. Bake, uncovered, at 325 degrees for 1 hour and 30 minutes. Beans may be topped with bacon slices before baking, if desired. 12 servings.

GOURMET LIMAS AND MUSHROOMS

1/2 lb. fresh mushrooms	1 tbsp. flour
Butter	2 c. cooked fresh lima beans
1 tbsp. finely chopped shallots	Salt and pepper to taste
1 c. light cream	

Clean and slice the mushrooms. Melt 2 tablespoons butter in a saucepan. Add the shallots and cook until soft. Add the mushrooms and cook until moisture has evaporated. Add the cream and cook until the liquid is reduced to 1/2 cup. Cream 1 tablespoon butter with the flour and add to the cream mixture, stirring to blend well. Add the lima beans and bring to a boil. Season with salt and pepper.

Mrs. Archie Dean, Frankfort, Kentucky

BUTTER BEANS IN SAVORY SAUCE

4 c. fresh butter beans	1/2 tsp. salt
2 sticks margarine	1/2 tsp. pepper
4 egg yolks	1/2 c. water
2 tbsp. grated onions	1/2 tsp. beef flavoring
2 tbsp. tarragon vinegar	

Place the butter beans in a saucepan and add 1 cup water. Bring to a boil and cook until tender. Add 1 stick margarine, stirring until melted. Beat the egg yolks thoroughly and place in a double boiler. Add the remaining margarine and all remaining ingredients except beans. Stir gently but constantly over low heat for 15 minutes or until sauce is of custard consistency. Serve over the butter beans. 6 servings.

Mrs. James T. Cook, Jr., Marianna, Florida

LIMAS IN PIQUANT SAUCE

4 c. fresh lima beans	1/4 tsp. pepper
2 c. water	4 tsp. prepared mustard
2 tsp. salt	1 c. milk
1/4 c. butter	4 tsp. lemon juice
1/4 c. flour	1/4 c. diced pimento

Combine the beans, water and 1 teaspoon salt in a saucepan. Bring to a boil and cook until tender. Drain and reserve liquid. Measure the liquid and add enough water to fill 1 cup. Melt the butter in a saucepan and blend in the flour, remaining salt and pepper. Stir in the mustard, bean liquid and milk. Cook until thickened, stirring constantly. Add the lemon juice and pimento. Pour the sauce over the beans. Heat and serve. 8 servings.

Mrs. Gene Taresh, Greenville, South Carolina

LIMA BEAN AND PEANUT ROAST

2 c. mashed potatoes	1/2 c. milk
2 1/2 c. cooked limas, drained	1 tsp. chopped onion
1 c. finely chopped, roasted	1 tsp. salt
peanuts	1/8 tsp. pepper
1 beaten egg	1/4 tsp. paprika

Place a layer of potatoes in a greased baking dish; add a layer of lima beans. Sprinkle with peanuts. Repeat layers until potatoes, beans and peanuts are used. Combine the remaining ingredients and pour over peanuts in dish. Bake in a 350-degree oven for 30 minutes. Serve with tomato or cheese sauce.

Maude Lee Patrick, Montgomery, Alabama

LIMA BEANS L'OIGNON

12 tiny onions
1/2 c. diced ham
Butter
1 tsp. flour
3 c. baby lima beans

3 or 4 lettuce leaves, shredded
1 c. water
1 tsp. salt
1 tbsp. chopped parsley

Saute the onions and ham in 2 tablespoons butter in a saucepan over low heat for about 4 minutes, stirring constantly. Stir in the flour, blending well. Add the lima beans, lettuce, water, salt and parsley. Cover the saucepan and bring the lima bean mixture to a boil. Lower the heat and cook for about 20 minutes or until the beans are tender. Stir in 3 tablespoons butter just before serving.

Mrs. Julie Daniel, Gadsden, Alabama

BLACK BEANS AND RICE

1 1/4 c. dried black beans
1 lge. onion, minced
2 garlic cloves
1 green pepper, chopped
1 carrot, sliced
2 whole cloves

1 bay leaf
1 tsp. salt
1/2 tsp. hot sauce
1/4 c. cooking oil
1/4 lb. smoked ham, chopped
4 c. hot cooked rice

Wash the beans thoroughly. Place in a 3-quart kettle or Dutch oven and add 1 quart water. Let stand overnight. Do not drain. Add the onion, reserving about 2 tablespoons for garnish. Add the garlic, green pepper, carrot, cloves, bay leaf, salt and hot sauce and simmer for about 1 hour or until beans are tender but whole. Heat the oil in a skillet. Add the reserved minced onion and ham and saute until lightly browned. Serve beans over rice and garnish with ham mixture. 4-6 servings.

Black Beans and Rice (above)

ALMOND BLACK EYES

2 1-lb. cans black-eyed peas
1/4 c. butter
1/4 c. coarsely chopped onion
1/3 c. (packed) brown sugar
1 tbsp. cornstarch

1/2 tsp. salt
1 1/2 tsp. vinegar
2 tsp. Worcestershire sauce
1/2 c. diced almonds, roasted

Drain the peas, reserving 1 cup liquid. Melt the butter in a medium saucepan. Add the onion and saute until tender-crisp. Stir in the brown sugar, cornstarch, salt and reserved liquid. Cook, stirring, until the mixture comes to a boil and is slightly thickened. Stir in the peas, vinegar, Worcestershire sauce and almonds. Heat in the saucepan or pour into 1-quart buttered casserole and cover. Bake in 375-degree oven for 20 minutes. 6 servings.

Mrs. Mamie Booker, Pensacola, Florida

BLACK-EYED PEAS DELICIOUS

1 lb. dried black-eyed peas
1 tbsp. salt
1 garlic clove, cut in half
1/2 c. oil
3 cloves of garlic, mashed
3 green peppers, chopped

3 med. onions, chopped
1/2 tsp. ground sage
2 bay leaves, crushed
3 tbsp. cider vinegar
1 tsp. salt
Pepper to taste

Wash and remove imperfect peas. Cover the peas with water and soak overnight, then drain. Place in a saucepan and cover with fresh water. Add the salt and garlic halves. Cook the peas for 3 hours or until tender, adding water as needed. Remove and discard the garlic halves. Heat the oil in a skillet and add the mashed garlic, green peppers, onions, sage and bay leaves. Cook until vegetables are soft. Add vinegar, salt and pepper to taste. Pour vegetable mixture into cooked peas. Blend and serve. 6-8 servings.

Mrs. Billy J. Hammond, Staples, Texas

HOPPING JOHN

1 8-oz. package black-eyed peas
1/2 lb. hambone
1 sm. onion, chopped
1 tsp. salt

1/4 tsp. pepper
1 c. instant rice
1 1-lb. can tomatoes

Place the peas in a large saucepan and cover with water. Bring to a boil and add the hambone, onion, salt and pepper. Cook for 1 hour and 15 minutes. Place the rice on top and add enough water to cover rice. Bring to boiling point and cover, then remove from heat. Let stand until rice is tender, then add tomatoes. 6 servings.

Mrs. Malta O. Ledford, Jupiter, Florida

BLACK-EYED PEAS AND FRESH OKRA

2 lb. fresh black-eyed peas
Salt pork

1 lb. fresh okra
Salt and pepper to taste

Shell the peas and place in a heavy saucepan. Cover with water and add salt pork. Bring to a boil and cook until tender. Wash the okra and place on top of the peas. Place the cover on the saucepan and remove from heat. Allow the okra to cook in the steam until barely tender. Season with salt and pepper.

Mrs. Patrick Sherlin, Charleston, South Carolina

TEXAS CAVIAR

2 No. 2 cans black-eyed peas
1/3 c. peanut oil
1/3 c. wine vinegar
1 clove of garlic

1/4 c. finely chopped onion
1/2 tsp. salt
Cracked pepper to taste

Drain the peas and place in a bowl. Add the oil, vinegar, garlic, onion, salt and pepper and mix well. Store in the refrigerator for 24 hours, then remove the garlic. Let set in the refrigerator for 2 days to 2 weeks before serving.

Mrs. Rachel Pearce, Fort Worth, Texas

LENTILS AND SAUSAGE

1 1/2 c. lentils
1 lge. onion, sliced
2 carrots, sliced
1 pkg. frozen Swiss chard

1 bay leaf
1 tsp. salt
Dash of pepper
1 smoked pork sausage ring

Rinse the lentils thoroughly. Place the lentils, onion, carrots, chard, seasonings and 2 cups boiling water in a saucepan and bring to a boil. Lower heat and simmer for 30 minutes. Add the sausage and cook for 20 to 30 minutes longer. Remove to serving platter. Slice sausage and place in overlapping rows on top. 6 to 8 servings.

Mrs. Virginia Jones, Villa Rica, Georgia

HEARTY LENTIL CASSEROLE

2 c. lentils, washed
1 lb. ground beef
1/2 c. salad oil
1 c. catsup

1 env. onion soup mix
1 tsp. cider vinegar
1 tsp. prepared mustard
1/8 tsp. pepper

Combine the lentils and 1 quart water in a saucepan. Cook, uncovered, over medium heat for 30 minutes. Brown the ground beef in oil. Stir in the lentils, catsup, soup mix, vinegar, mustard, pepper and 1 cup water. Pour into a 2 1/2-quart casserole. Bake, uncovered, at 400 degrees for 30 minutes. 8 servings.

Mrs. Anna San Juan, Pecos, New Mexico

COUNTRY-STYLE CASSOULET

2 lb. dried pea navy beans
1/4 lb. salt pork, diced
1 c. chopped onions
1   10 1/2-oz. can tomato puree
2 carrots, sliced
4 cloves of garlic, minced
2 lb. smoked pork butt, sliced

1 1/2 lb. Chorizo or Spanish-style
   sausage
1   4 3/4-oz. jar pimento-stuffed
   olives
1/2 tsp. pepper
1   4 to 5-lb. duckling with giblets
1 tsp. salt

Cover the beans with water and soak overnight. Drain. Place in a large kettle and cover with salted water. Bring to a boil and boil for 2 minutes. Let stand, uncovered, for 30 minutes. Fry the salt pork in a skillet until partially done. Add onions, tomato puree, carrots and garlic and simmer for about 15 minutes or until onions are tender. Add to beans along with pork butt and Chorizo. Drain and slice the olives and add to bean mixture. Add the pepper and cover. Cook for 2 hours and 30 minutes to 3 hours or until beans are tender, stirring occasionally. Add the giblets and salt to 1 cup boiling water and cover. Simmer until tender. Chop the giblets and add with giblet liquid to beans. Rinse the duckling with cold water and prick with a fork. Place on a rack in a baking pan. Roast in 350-degree oven for 2 hours or until done. Slice the duckling. Place alternate layers of bean mixture and meats in a casserole. Bake in 350-degree oven for 1 to 2 hours, stirring occasionally. Season 1 1/2 pounds ground pork with 1 1/2 teaspoons chili powder, 1 tablespoon salt and 1 tablespoon vinegar if Chorizo is not available. Shape into patties and brown before adding to beans. 8-10 servings.

Country-Style Cassoulet (above)

45

SOYBEAN LOAF

1 c. soybeans	1/2 c. cream
1 sm. onion	2 eggs, slightly beaten
1 c. ground walnuts	1 tbsp. butter or vegetable oil
1 c. toasted bread crumbs	Salt to taste

Soak the soybeans in water to cover overnight or longer. Drain and cover the soybeans with fresh water. Cook for 2 hours or until tender, then add the onion. Cook until well done and mash the beans until smooth. Add remaining ingredients and mix well. Press the soybean mixture into a baking dish. Bake at 350 to 400 degrees for 45 minutes. Serve with cranberry or other tart jelly. 8 servings.

Mrs. Mary Teaberry, Springfield, Kentucky

SOYBEAN CASSEROLE

1/4 c. diced salt pork	2 c. milk
2 c. chopped celery	1 tbsp. salt
2 tbsp. chopped onions	2 c. chopped cooked soybeans
2 tbsp. chopped green pepper	1 c. buttered bread crumbs
6 tbsp. sifted flour	1/2 tsp. paprika

Cook the salt pork in a frying pan until brown. Add the celery, onions and green pepper and stir and cook for 5 minutes. Blend the flour with milk and salt in a saucepan and bring to a boil, stirring constantly. Add the soybeans and celery mixture and pour into a casserole. Cover with crumbs and sprinkle with paprika. Bake at 350 degrees for 30 minutes.

Dicy Fox, Dandridge, Tennessee

COMPANY'S SOYBEANS

2 c. dried soybeans	1 lge. diced onion
6 c. water	1/2 c. diced celery
1 sm. ham hock	3 bay leaves
2 tbsp. honey or molasses	Salt to taste

Soak the soybeans in water overnight or for 24 hours, then drain off water and rinse well. Add remaining ingredients and cover well with additional water. Bring to a boil, then lower heat. Simmer for 3 hours or until tender. May be cooked in pressure saucepan for 30 minutes at 10 pounds pressure if desired.

Mrs. Dotson G. Lewis, Fayetteville, Arkansas

GREEN PEAS FLORENTINE PIE

8 bacon slices, diced	1/2 c. milk
1 1/2 c. thinly sliced onions	1/2 tsp. salt
1 10-oz. package frozen green	3 eggs, slightly beaten
peas and celery	Cheese Crust
1/2 c. light cream	

Saute the bacon in a skillet until crisp. Remove from skillet and drain on absorbent paper. Saute the onions in bacon drippings in the skillet until tender but not browned. Remove from skillet and drain on absorbent paper. Cook the peas and celery according to package directions. Place the cream, milk and salt in a saucepan and bring to a boil. Pour a small amount of milk mixture into eggs, stirring constantly. Stir back into milk mixture in saucepan, then stir in the peas and celery, onions and bacon. Pour into the Cheese Crust. Bake at 400 degrees for 15 minutes. Reduce temperature to 325 degrees and bake for 15 minutes longer or until a knife inserted 1 inch from center of pie comes out clean. Center will be soft. Cool for several minutes before serving.

Cheese Crust

1 c. grated Cheddar cheese	1/4 tsp. dry mustard
3/4 c. flour	1/4 c. melted butter

Combine all ingredients in a bowl and mix thoroughly. Press firmly on bottom and side of a 9-inch pie pan.

Green Peas Florentine Pie (above)

AMANDINE PEAS AND ONIONS

1 10-oz. package frozen English peas	1/2 c. melted butter
1 c. diagonally cut celery	1 sm. can whole onions
1/2 c. slivered blanched almonds	Salt and pepper to taste

Prepare the peas according to package directions. Cook the celery in boiling salted water until tender but crisp, then drain. Brown almonds lightly in butter and add the onions, peas and celery. Season with salt and pepper. Serve hot. 8-10 servings.

Mrs. Bob Yarbrough, Birmingham, Alabama

CASSEROLE OF PEAS

1 No. 2 can peas	1 tbsp. flour
2 hard-cooked eggs, chopped	1 tbsp. butter
1/4 tsp. salt	1 c. buttered cracker crumbs
Pepper	1/2 c. grated cheese

Drain the peas, reserving juice. Place the peas in a buttered casserole. Add the eggs and seasonings. Make a paste with a small amount of the reserved juice and the flour. Pour remaining liquid from peas into a saucepan and heat. Add the flour paste and cook, stirring constantly, until thickened. Add the butter and pour over the peas. Brown the buttered crumbs slightly. Mix crumbs with the cheese and pour over peas. Bake for 30 minutes at 350 degrees. 6 servings.

Mrs. Norma Wilson, Mobile, Alabama

CURRIED PECAN AND GREEN PEA SHORTCAKES

2 c. prepared biscuit mix	1 10-oz. package frozen peas, partially thawed
1/3 c. soft butter	1/2 tsp. salt
2/3 c. milk	1 c. broken pecans
2 tbsp. finely chopped onion	
3 tbsp. water	

Combine biscuit mix, 1/4 cup butter and milk according to package directions. Roll 1/4 inch thick on lightly floured surface, then cut with a 3-inch biscuit cutter. Cut centers from half of the rounds with a 1 1/2-inch cutter or knife. Stack biscuits with center holes atop biscuit rounds. Place on a baking sheet. Bake as directed on biscuit mix package. Place the onion in a saucepan with remaining butter and cover. Cook until tender, then add water, peas and salt. Cover and cook over low heat until peas are tender. Stir in the pecans and heat.

Sauce

2 tbsp. butter or margarine	1/2 tsp. curry powder
2 tbsp. flour	1/2 c. half and half
1/2 tsp. salt	3/4 c. milk
1/2 tsp. paprika	

Melt the butter, then stir in flour, salt, paprika and curry powder. Add half and half and milk. Cook, stirring constantly, until smooth and thickened. Fill the holes in each biscuit with pea mixture and top with sauce. 4 servings.

Mrs. Tony Fisher, Bayard, New Mexico

PEAS CHAMBOURD

1 17-oz. can peas with onions	Dash of pepper
1/2 c. catsup	1/3 c. grated Parmesan cheese
1/2 tsp. salt	

Drain the peas and onions and combine with the catsup, salt and pepper in a greased casserole. Sprinkle with the cheese. Bake at 350 degrees for 20 minutes. 4 servings.

Mrs. Karen Williams, Zachary, Louisiana

POLE BEANS WITH MUSTARD SAUCE

1 1/2 lb. fresh Florida pole beans	1 tbsp. prepared mustard
1/2 tsp. salt	1/4 tsp. lemon juice
1 3/4-oz. package white sauce mix	2 tbsp. diced pimento

Remove tips from pole beans and cut beans into 1-inch pieces. Bring 1 inch water and salt to boiling point in a medium saucepan. Add the beans and cook for 5 minutes. Reduce heat and cover. Simmer for 10 minutes or until beans are crisp-tender. Drain. Prepare sauce mix according to package directions. Add the mustard and lemon juice and mix well. Stir in the pimento. Place the beans in a serving bowl. Serve with sauce spooned over top. 6 servings.

Pole Beans with Mustard Sauce (above)

HERBED PEAS

1/2 c. sliced green onion	1/2 tsp. salt
2 tbsp. butter	1/8 tsp. pepper
2 10-oz. packages frozen green	1/4 tsp. basil
peas	1 tbsp. parsley flakes
1/2 tsp. sugar	

Saute the onion in the butter in a saucepan until soft, then add the frozen peas and 1/4 cup water. Bring to a boil, then stir in remaining ingredients. Simmer, covered, for 10 minutes. 4-6 servings.

Sister Mary Albertus, S.S.N.D., Tyler, Texas

FROZEN PEAS IN CREAM

1 pkg. green peas	Sugar to taste
1/2 to 1 c. cream	Butter to taste
Salt and pepper to taste	

Partially cook the peas and drain. Combine the cream, salt and pepper, sugar and butter in the top of a double boiler. Heat, stirring until well-mixed, then add the peas. Cook, covered, over boiling water for 15 to 30 minutes or until tender. 4 servings.

Betty Anne Cobble, Hohenwald, Tennessee

PIQUANT YULE PEAS

1 No. 2 can English peas	1 sm. can pimento strips
1 can mushrooms	1 can tomato soup
1 c. grated American cheese	1 tsp. Worcestershire sauce
1 c. chili sauce	6 hard-cooked eggs, sliced
1 green pepper, chopped	1 1/2 c. white sauce
fine	Butter
1 c. finely chopped celery	

Mix all ingredients except eggs, white sauce and butter. Place half the vegetable mixture in a greased baking dish. Add half the eggs, then half the white sauce. Repeat layers and dot with butter. Bake at 350 degrees for 20 to 30 minutes. 6-8 servings.

Mrs. Clara Comer, Florence, Alabama

PEAS AND HAM CURRY

1 1-lb. 1-oz. can sweet peas	1/4 tsp. monosodium glutamate
1/4 lb. cooked cubed ham	2 tbsp. flour
2 tbsp. butter	1/4 tsp. salt
1/2 tsp. curry powder	1 c. milk

Drain the peas and combine with ham in a 1 1/2-quart casserole. Blend the butter, curry powder, monosodium glutamate, flour and salt. Stir in the milk and cook until thickened, stirring constantly. Remove from heat and fold into peas and ham. Bake, covered, at 325 degrees for 30 minutes. 4 servings.

Patricia A. Glass, Dill City, Oklahoma

PEAS AND RICE WITH EGGS

2 c. cooked rice	**Grated cheese**
1 c. cooked peas	**Salt to taste**
4 tbsp. melted butter	**4 to 6 eggs**

Combine the rice and peas. Add the butter, 1/4 cup grated cheese and salt. Spread the mixture in a shallow baking dish. Make 4 to 6 small wells and break an egg in each. Sprinkle with salt and grated cheese. Bake in 350-degree oven until eggs are set and cheese is melted.

Mrs. Marvin Leifeste, Mason, Texas

DIXIE POLE BEANS

1 lb. fresh Florida pole beans	**1/2 tsp. crumbled basil leaves**
3 strips bacon	**1/2 tsp. salt**
1/2 c. finely chopped onion	**Dash of red pepper**
1 chicken bouillon cube	**1 1/2 tsp. cornstarch**

Trim stem ends from beans and cut into 2-inch pieces. Saute the bacon in a large skillet until crisp. Remove bacon and crumble. Add the onion to bacon fat and saute for 2 minutes. Add the beans, 3/4 cup water, bouillon cube, basil, salt and red pepper and cover the skillet. Simmer for 15 minutes. Mix the cornstarch with 1/4 cup water and stir into beans mixture. Cook until thickened and clear. Sprinkle bacon over beans. 6 servings.

Dixie Pole Beans (above)

PEA TIMBALES

1 1/2 c. pea puree
2 tbsp. melted butter

3 eggs, well beaten
Salt and pepper

Blend all the ingredients well and pour into greased molds. Set the molds in a pan of hot water. Bake at 250 to 325 degrees until set. May be served with white sauce. 6-8 servings.

Katherine Potter, Scurry, Texas

GREEN BEANS

4 lb. tender green beans
1 tsp. salt

1 sm. piece of salt pork

Snap the ends from the green beans and remove any strings. Break into 2-inch lengths and place in a saucepan. Cover with water and add the salt and salt pork. Bring to a boil, then reduce heat. Simmer for about 1 hour or until the beans are tender. Three to 4 tablespoons bacon fat may be substituted for salt pork, if desired.

Mrs. Aubrey W. Walker, Oxford, Mississippi

GREEN BEAN BOUQUET

2 lb. tender green beans
2 tsp. salt
1 stick butter

2 tbsp. chopped pimentos
White pepper to taste

Wash the beans well. Cut off ends and split lengthwise. Let stand in ice water for about 1 hour. Tie the beans in small bunches with string. Place in a saucepan and cook in boiling salted water until just tender. Drain well, then place in a serving dish. Melt the butter in a saucepan and add pimentos. Pour over the beans. Sprinkle with the white pepper and serve.

Mrs. Winthrop Rockefeller, Little Rock, Arkansas

BEAN CASSEROLE

2 cans French-style green beans
2 tbsp. butter
3 tbsp. flour
1 tbsp. instant minced onion
1 tbsp. sugar
1 tsp. salt

Pepper to taste
1 lb. Swiss cheese, grated
1 sm. can pimento strips
1 pt. sour cream
3/4 c. crushed corn flakes

Drain the beans and place in a casserole. Melt the butter in a saucepan and stir in the flour. Add the onion, sugar, salt, pepper, cheese, pimento and sour cream and cook over low heat until cheese is melted. Remove from heat. Pour over the beans and sprinkle with corn flakes. Bake at 375 degrees for 15 minutes or until bubbly.

Mrs. Gladys Hinchey, Dandridge, Tennessee

PENNSYLVANIA DUTCH-STYLE GREEN BEANS

3 strips bacon	1 No. 303 can green beans
1 sm. onion, sliced	1 tbsp. brown sugar
2 tsp. cornstarch	1 tbsp. vinegar
1/4 tsp. salt	1 hard-cooked egg, sliced
1/4 tsp. dry mustard	

Fry the bacon in a skillet until crisp. Remove and crumble the bacon. Pour off all but 1 tablespoon of the drippings. Add the onion and brown lightly. Stir in the cornstarch, salt and mustard. Drain the beans, reserving 1/2 cup liquid. Pour the bean liquid into the skillet. Cook, stirring, until the mixture comes to a boil. Blend in the brown sugar and vinegar; add the beans. Heat thoroughly. Turn into a serving dish and garnish with the egg and crumbled bacon. 4 servings.

Mrs. Lucille C. Duncan, Willis, Virginia

SALADE JARDINIERE

1 1-lb. can whole baby carrots	1 1-lb. can garbanzos or chick-peas
1 1-lb. can hearts of palm	1/2 c. thinly sliced scallions
	3/4 c. creole French dressing

Drain the carrots, hearts of palm and garbanzos. Reserve half the carrots and slice lengthwise. Slice remaining carrots lengthwise, then into 1-inch pieces. Cut hearts of palm into 1/4-inch slices and reserve half the slices. Combine the carrots, hearts of palm, garbanzos and scallions in a large bowl. Add the creole French dressing and mix lightly. Refrigerate for 2 to 3 hours or overnight. Mound on a salad platter. Decorate rim of salad platter with alternating slices of reserved hearts of palm and carrot slices. Garnish with parsley sprigs. 6-8 servings.

Salade Jardiniere (above)

GREEN BEANS WITH ORANGES

2 10-oz. packages frozen whole green beans	3 tbsp. butter
1 11-oz. can mandarin oranges	Salt and pepper to taste

Cook beans according to package directions and drain. Drain the oranges and add to the beans. Add the butter and heat through. Season with salt and pepper. 6 servings.

Mrs. Henry Finch, Dallas, Georgia

GREEN BEAN-PINEAPPLE VINAIGRETTE

1 9-oz. package frozen Italian green beans	1/4 tsp. dried dill
	1/8 tsp. hot sauce
1 20-oz. can pineapple chunks	1/4 tsp. garlic salt
1 12-oz. jar sweet mixed pickles	1 sm. green pepper
1/2 c. wine vinegar	1 c. thinly sliced celery
1/4 c. salad oil	1 lge. tomato

Cook beans until tender but crisp and drain. Cool. Drain the pineapple and pickles and reserve 1/3 cup syrup from each. Combine the syrups and blend with the vinegar, oil, dill, hot sauce and salt. Cut the green pepper in strips. Combine the beans, pineapple, pickles, green pepper and celery in a bowl and add the dressing. Chill, covered, for several hours. Cut the tomato in wedges. Garnish the green bean mixture with the tomato wedges and serve cold. 10 servings.

Ardis Boyd, Louisville, Kentucky

GREEN BEAN CASSEROLE

1 can seasoned green beans	1 sm. jar pimento strips
1 sm. can water chestnuts, sliced	1 can cream of mushroom soup
	1 can French-fried onion rings

Cook the beans according to can directions and drain. Add the water chestnuts, pimento and soup and mix well. Place in a 1 1/2-quart casserole and top with onion rings. Bake at 350 degrees for 10 minutes or until onion rings are brown. 6-8 servings.

Jean E. McDonald, Hartford, Alabama

DILLED GREEN BEANS

1/3 c. red wine vinegar	1/4 tsp. salt
1/4 c. Burgundy	Dash of garlic powder
1/2 tsp. Beau Monde seasoning	3 tbsp. olive oil
1 tsp. dried dill	1 No. 303 can whole green
1 tbsp. instant minced onion	beans, drained

Mix all ingredients except the beans in a saucepan and heat through. Pour over the beans in a bowl and chill thoroughly, stirring occasionally.

Mrs. George Evans, Pensacola, Florida

GARBANZO BEAN SURPRISE

1 lb. garbanzo beans	2 tbsp. chopped parsley
1 c. chopped onions	2 tbsp. pine nuts
3 tbsp. olive oil	Sesame seed oil

Place the beans in a saucepan and cover with cold water, then cover the saucepan. Allow the beans to soak overnight. Bring to a boil and simmer the beans until tender. Drain and grind the beans to a fine paste. Saute the onions in the olive oil until the onion is tender. Stir in the parsley and pine nuts and then mix well with paste. Chill and drizzle with a small amount of oil. Serve cold.

Mrs. Helen Reed, San Antonio, Texas

MIXED BEAN SALAD

1 20-oz. can red kidney beans	1/3 c. wine vinegar
1 16-oz. can pinto beans	1/8 tsp. instant minced
1/2 c. chopped green onions	garlic
1 tbsp. chopped parsley	Salt and pepper to taste
1/2 c. olive or salad oil	Lettuce

Drain the beans, then rinse and drain again. Combine the beans, onions and parsley in a bowl. Blend the oil with vinegar and garlic. Pour over the bean mixture and mix lightly. Season with salt and pepper and chill. Serve in a lettuce-lined bowl. 6 servings.

Mixed Bean Salad (above)

GARBANZO BEAN SALAD

1/2 lb. dried garbanzo beans	1/2 c. pimento-stuffed olives
1/2 c. tarragon vinegar	1/4 lb. hard salami
1/4 c. olive oil	Salad greens
1 clove of garlic, crushed	3 tbsp. finely chopped scallions
1/2 tsp. salt	or green onions
Dash of pepper	2 tomatoes, diced

Soak the beans in cold water overnight and drain. Cover with salted water in a saucepan. Bring to a boil and simmer for 1 hour and 45 minutes or until tender. Drain and rinse with cold water. Drain again. Combine the vinegar, oil, garlic, salt and pepper in a bowl. Slice the olives and cut the salami into strips. Add the beans, olives and salami to the vinegar mixture. Mix lightly and chill. Line a bowl with the salad greens and add the chilled salad. Sprinkle with the scallions and garnish with the tomatoes. 6 servings.

Mrs. Laura Roth, Fields, Louisiana

FRIJOLES

2 lb. pinto beans	2 lge. onions
2 tsp. salt	4 garlic cloves
1/2 tsp. cumin	Hambone or ham trimmings
1/2 can tomatoes and green chilies	1 tsp. chili powder

Cover the beans with water in a saucepan. Cook slowly until skins burst. Add remaining ingredients and cook for 1 hour longer. Add water as needed.

Mrs. H. Richard Jones, Ruston, Louisiana

PINTO BEAN SALAD

1 No. 303 can pinto beans	3 hard-cooked eggs, chopped
3 med. sweet pickles	1/4 tsp. salt
1 sm. onion, chopped	2 tbsp. mayonnaise

Drain the liquid from the beans and mash. Chop the sweet pickles. Combine the beans, onion, eggs, sweet pickles and salt. Add the mayonnaise and toss lightly until all ingredients are coated. 6 servings.

Mrs. Kay Garrison, Red Bay, Alabama

BAKED PINTO BEANS

3 1/2 c. cooked pinto beans	1/2 c. chopped green pepper
1 lge. onion, chopped	1/2 c. brown sugar

1/2 tsp. salt
3/4 c. catsup

1 tsp. prepared mustard
6 strips (about) bacon, diced

Combine all the ingredients and place in a bean pot. Lay additional strips of bacon across top. Bake at 375 degrees for 1 hour and 30 minutes. 8-10 servings.

Mrs. Arthur Robinson, Alameda, New Mexico

HOT BEANS

3 slices bacon
2 med. onions
3 tbsp. catsup
2 tbsp. red hot sauce

2 tbsp. Worcestershire sauce
Salt and pepper to taste
8 o. oooked pinto beans

Dice the bacon and fry until brown in a Dutch oven. Remove half the bacon grease and add the onions to the bacon, cooking until done. Add remaining ingredients and simmer slowly for about 30 minutes, stirring occasionally. 8-10 servings.

Mrs. Dwight Moody, Goldonna, Louisiana

BEAN POT PINTOS

2 c. dried pinto beans
5 c. water
1 sm. piece of salt pork
1 sm. onion, chopped

1 6-oz. cola beverage
1/2 tsp. salt
5 dried chili peppers

Combine the beans, water, salt pork and onion in a bean pot and cook overnight. Add the cola beverage, salt and chili peppers and cook for several hours longer. 8 servings.

Mrs. Eleanor Weatherman, Wink, Texas

MEXICAN-STYLE PINTO BEANS

2 lb. pinto beans
2 tsp. salt
1 can roasted green chilies
2 lge. onions, diced
4 cloves of garlic, diced

1/2 tsp. pepper
1/2 tsp. comino seed
1 can taco sauce
2 c. tomatoes

Soak the beans overnight in cold water, then drain. Cover with water and add salt. Boil for 1 hour. Chop the green chilies. Add the onions, garlic, pepper, comino seed, green chilies, taco sauce and tomatoes to the pinto beans. Cook for 1 hour and 30 minutes. 30 servings.

Mrs. Howard Merhoff, Newkirk, Oklahoma

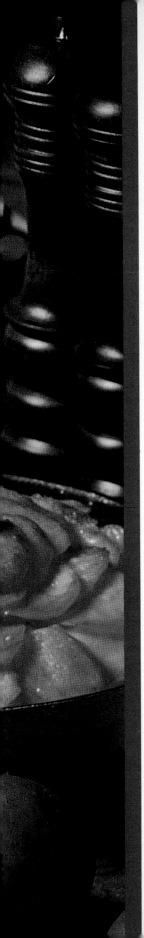

root vegetables

Root vegetables — especially potatoes — are an important part of everyone's diet. And the recipes awaiting you in the section which follows offer you new and exciting ways to serve these standbys.

For example, your family probably enjoys potatoes baked and mashed. Combine the two cooking methods and feature unusual Baked Mashed Potatoes at dinner tonight — then sit back and enjoy the compliments! Or introduce an Italian note into your family's dining with Gnocchi, tiny potato dumplings which Italians around New Orleans often serve with spicy meat sauce.

Sweet potatoes are popular fare in homes throughout the South — no Thanksgiving dinner would be complete without them. Treat your family to traditional Candied Sweet Potatoes — or feature a time-treasured recipe such as Sweet Potato Pudding of 1828.

But potatoes — sweet or otherwise — are not the only root vegetables southern homemakers have turned into delicious dishes. Beets are marvelous hot or cold — Baby Beets in Sour Cream and Beet Relish Salad both feature this brightly-colored vegetable in savory dishes! You'll discover these recipes and many more waiting for you in the pages of this section. These home-tested root vegetable dishes will bring new flavor excitement to every menu — try them and see!

59

BABY BEETS IN SOUR CREAM

1/4 c. sour cream	1/2 tsp. salt
1 tbsp. vinegar	Dash of cayenne
1 tsp. minced green onion	2 1/2 c. halved cooked beets
3/4 tsp. sugar	

Blend all the ingredients except the beets in a bowl. Drain the beets and place in a saucepan. Pour the sauce over the beets. Heat over low heat, stirring, until the beets are coated. 4-5 servings.

Mrs. Wilma Haring, Clayton, Georgia

BEETS WITH HONEY SAUCE

2 tbsp. butter or margarine	2 tbsp. light brown sugar
2 tbsp. flour	2 tsp. lemon juice
1 tbsp. honey	3 c. cooked beets

Melt the butter in a saucepan, then stir in the flour. Add the honey, sugar and lemon juice. Simmer. stirring constantly, until thickened and clear. Add the beets and heat through.

Maude E. Ramsdell, Columbia, South Carolina

BEET RELISH SALAD

1 3-oz. package lemon gelatin	1 1/2 c. canned diced beets, drained
1 1/4 c. hot water	1/2 c. diced celery
3/4 c. beet liquid	1 tsp. horseradish
2 tbsp. vinegar	1 tsp. Worcestershire sauce
1/2 tsp. salt	1 tsp. grated onion
	4 drops of hot sauce

Dissolve the gelatin in hot water in a bowl. Add the beet liquid, vinegar and 1/4 teaspoon salt and mix well. Chill until partially set. Add remaining salt and remaining ingredients and mix. Turn into individual molds and chill until firm. 12 servings.

Mrs. Frederick H. Horton, Indian Harbour Beach, Florida

BROWN SUGAR-HARVARD BEETS

1/2 c. brown sugar	1/4 c. vinegar
2 tbsp. cornstarch	1 No. 2 can diced beets, drained
1/2 tsp. salt	

Combine the sugar, cornstarch and salt in a saucepan. Add the vinegar and 1/4 cup water, stirring until well mixed. Cook over medium heat, until thickened, stirring constantly. Add the beets to the sauce and serve hot.

Mrs. Charlene Slack, East Bernard, Texas

BEETS WITH ORANGE SAUCE

1/2 c. sugar	1/4 c. orange juice
2 tsp. cornstarch	1 tbsp. butter
1 tsp. orange rind	1 No. 303 can beets
1 tbsp. lemon juice	

Combine the sugar and cornstarch in a saucepan. Add 1/2 cup boiling water and cook for 15 minutes. Add the orange rind, lemon juice, orange juice and butter. Pour the beets into a saucepan and bring to a boil, then drain. Remove the beets to a serving dish and spoon the orange sauce over the beets. Serve hot. 5 servings.

Mrs. Shirley Flynn, Hot Springs, Virginia

BOILED DINNER BEETS

1 lb. fresh sm. whole beets	2 tbsp. melted butter
1 lb. fresh whole onions	1/4 c. lemon gelatin

Trim the beets. Cook in boiling, salted water until tender. Drain and reserve 1/4 cup liquid. Cool and peel. Peel the onions and cook in boiling, salted water until tender. Drain. Mix the reserved liquid with the butter and gelatin in a saucepan and bring to a boil, stirring constantly. Add the onions and beets and heat through. 6 servings.

Boiled Dinner Beets (above)

BAKED CARROTS

1 lb. carrots	**1 tsp. salt**
1/3 c. butter	**1/3 tsp. cinnamon**
1/2 c. sugar	

Scrape the carrots. Leave small carrots whole and slice large carrots. Place in a casserole. Cream the butter, sugar, salt and cinnamon together. Add 1 cup boiling water and blend well. Pour over the carrots and cover. Bake in 350-degree oven for 1 hour and 30 minutes. 6-8 servings.

Mrs. James K. Cortner, Wartrace, Tennessee

BAKED APPLE AND CARROT CASSEROLE

5 apples, thinly sliced	**2 tbsp. flour**
2 c. cooked sliced carrots	**Salt to taste**
6 tbsp. sugar	**3/4 c. orange juice**

Place a layer of apple slices in a baking dish, then cover with a layer of carrots. Mix the sugar, flour and salt and sprinkle over the carrots. Repeat layers and pour juice over all. Bake at 350 degrees for 20 to 30 minutes. 5 servings.

Mrs. Junnie M. Goldston, Leaksville, North Carolina

CARROTS IN PARSLEY BUTTER

8 med. carrots	**2 tbsp. lemon juice**
1/2 tsp. salt	**1 tbsp. chopped parsley**
1/4 c. butter	

Wash and scrape the carrots, then cut in slices into a saucepan. Add a small amount of water and bring to a boil. Cook for 10 to 15 minutes or until tender. Drain and add salt, butter, lemon juice and parsley. Serve hot.

Mrs. Joe T. Ipock, Newbern, North Carolina

CARROT LOAF

1/2 c. bread crumbs	**1/2 tsp. salt**
2 1/2 c. mashed cooked carrots	**1 tsp. finely chopped onion**
2 eggs	**1 1/2 tsp. butter**
1 c. milk	**3/4 c. chopped peanuts**
1 tsp. sugar	

Combine the crumbs and carrots. Beat the eggs and milk together. Add the egg mixture and remaining ingredients to the carrots. Turn into greased molds or shallow dish and set in a pan of water. Bake at 350 degrees for 30 minutes. Remove from molds or cut in squares to serve. 8 servings.

Sara Hancock, Florence, Alabama

CARROT FRITTERS

6 cooked med. carrots	**1 egg**
1/2 c. sugar	**1 tsp. vanilla**
Dash of salt	**1 1/2 c. plain flour**
2 tsp. baking powder	

Mash the carrots until smooth and combine with remaining ingredients. Drop by spoonfuls into deep 370-degree fat. Fry for about 3 minutes or until brown. Turn and brown the other side. Drain and serve hot.

Mrs. Lloyd L. Boquet, Bourg, Louisiana

CARROTS AND CLOVES

12 sm. carrots, peeled	**6 whole cloves**
1 6-oz. can frozen lemonade	

Boil the carrots in a small amount of water in a saucepan until tender. Drain and add lemonade and cloves. Simmer over low heat for 5 minutes. Chill thoroughly, then drain. Serve on lettuce.

Mrs. Lou Ann Simpson, Glasgow, Kentucky

PARSLEYED FRESH CARROTS

8 med. fresh carrots	**1 tsp. sugar**
1 c. bouillon	**1/2 tsp. salt**
3 tbsp. butter or margarine	**2 tsp. chopped fresh parsley**

Scrape the carrots and cut in 3/4-inch pieces. Place in a saucepan. Add the bouillon, butter, sugar and salt and bring to a boil. Reduce heat and cover. Simmer for 25 to 30 minutes or until carrots are tender. Place in a bowl and sprinkle with parsley.

Parsleyed Fresh Carrots (above)

Bountiful Vegetable Platter (below)

BOUNTIFUL VEGETABLE PLATTER

8 lge. Bermuda onions	2 16-oz. cans baby whole
2 8-oz. packages frozen	carrots
green peas with cream sauce	1/4 c. finely chopped parsley
2 strips bacon, diced	1/4 c. melted butter
2 slices bread, diced	

Peel the onions and scoop out centers, leaving a shell about 3/4 inch thick. Place in boiling, salted water and simmer until onions are tender but still hold shape. Leave in hot water. Cook the peas according to package directions. Fry the bacon in a skillet until crisp. Remove from skillet and drain. Add the bread cubes to bacon drippings in the skillet and fry until brown and crisp. Heat the carrots in a saucepan, then drain and toss with parsley and butter. Place the onions on a platter. Fill with peas and top with bacon and croutons. Surround onions with carrots. Serve at once.

COPPER CARROT PENNIES

2 lb. carrots, sliced	1 c. sugar
1 sm. green pepper	3/4 c. vinegar
1 med. onion, thinly sliced	1 tsp. prepared mustard
1 can tomato soup	1 tsp. Worcestershire sauce
1/2 c. salad oil	Salt and pepper to taste

Boil the carrots in salted water in a saucepan until fork tender. Set aside to cool. Cut green pepper in rings. Alternate layers of carrots, pepper rings and onion slices in a dish. Combine the remaining ingredients and beat until well blended. Pour mixture over vegetables and refrigerate until serving time. Keeps well in the refrigerator. 12-15 servings.

Mrs. Juanita Williams, Graceville, Florida

CREAMY CARROT SOUFFLE

2 c. shredded carrots	1 tsp. instant minced onion
1/2 tsp. salt	1/4 tsp. cream of tartar
3 eggs, separated	1/8 tsp. nutmeg
1 c. thick white sauce	

Place the carrots and 2 tablespoons salted water in a saucepan and cover. Bring to a boil and cook over low heat until tender. Beat egg yolks until well blended, then add white sauce slowly, stirring until smooth. Blend in the carrots and onion. Beat egg whites with cream of tartar until stiff. Fold into carrot mixture. Pour into a greased 1 1/2-quart casserole and sprinkle with nutmeg. Place in a pan of hot water. Bake for 40 minutes at 350 degrees. 6 servings.

Aunean Brown, Tioga, Texas

GOLDEN CARROTS

3 c. sliced cooked carrots	1 tsp. tapioca
1 No. 303 can pineapple bits	1/2 tsp. salt
2 tbsp. brown sugar	1 tsp. butter

Place the carrots in a buttered baking dish. Drain the pineapple bits and reserve the juice. Add the pineapple to the carrots and mix well. Combine the reserved juice with the brown sugar, tapioca and salt, stirring until dissolved. Pour over the carrot mixture and dot with butter. Cover. Bake for 30 minutes in a 350-degree oven.

Mrs. Julian Carpenter, Landrum, South Carolina

BEEFY ONION RINGS

1 beef bouillon cube	1 egg
1/2 c. boiling water	Cooking oil
1 c. pancake mix	1 onion, cut into rings

Dissolve the bouillon cube in boiling water and cool. Beat the pancake mix with the egg, 1 tablespoon cooking oil and bouillon. Dip the onion rings in the batter and drain slightly. Fry in 1 inch of oil heated to 350 degrees for 3 minutes, turning once.

Mrs. Clara Maples, Sweeny, Texas

ONIONS BURGUNDIAN

6 lge. yellow onions	Salt and pepper to taste
3 tbsp. butter	1 c. Burgundy
2 whole cloves	

Slice the onions 1/4 inch thick and separate into rings. Melt the butter in a large skillet. Add the onions and saute, stirring, until golden brown. Add the cloves, salt, pepper and Burgundy and cover. Simmer for 15 minutes. Remove cover and simmer until liquid is nearly evaporated, stirring frequently.

Mrs. Iris Stockton, New Castle, Delaware

GLAZED WHOLE ONIONS

3 lb. white onions, peeled	1/2 tsp. salt
4 tsp. sugar	6 tbsp. melted butter
1 tsp. dry mustard	1/4 tsp. paprika

Place the onions in a saucepan and add about 2 cups water. Bring to a boil and lower the heat. Simmer for 20 to 30 minutes or until the onions are tender, then drain. Arrange the onions in a shallow baking dish. Combine the remaining ingredients and pour over the onions. Bake at 325 degrees for 20 minutes, basting occasionally. 6 servings.

Mrs. Marguerite McGinness, Danbury, Texas

CREAMED ONIONS WITH PEANUTS

2 tbsp. butter	1 1/2 c. milk
1 1/2 tbsp. flour	2 c. cooked sliced onions
1/2 tsp. salt	1/2 c. chopped salted peanuts
Pepper to taste	1/4 c. dry bread crumbs

Melt 1 tablespoon butter in a saucepan and blend in flour and seasonings. Add the milk and cook over low heat, stirring constantly, until thickened. Alternate layers of onions, peanuts and sauce in baking dish. Melt the remaining butter and combine with bread crumbs. Sprinkle over the top layer. Bake at 400 degrees for 20 minutes. 4 servings.

Mrs. Josephine Kelm, Morgantown, Kentucky

CREAMED ONIONS WITH MUSHROOMS

2 tbsp. butter	2 tbsp. chopped parsley
2 tbsp. flour	10 med. onions, cooked
1 c. milk	1/2 c. mushrooms
1/4 tsp. salt	1/2 tsp. grated lemon rind
1/8 tsp. paprika	Juice of 1 lemon

Melt the butter in a saucepan and blend in the flour. Add the milk gradually, stirring until smooth. Cook until thickened, stirring constantly. Add the salt, paprika and parsley. Combine onions, mushrooms, lemon rind and juice and add the sauce. Serve hot. 6 servings.

Mrs. Anna Benda Whitescarver, Flemington, West Virginia

ISLAND-INSPIRED ONIONS

8 med. onions	2 tbsp. brown sugar
1 tbsp. butter	1 tsp. cornstarch
1 15 1/2-oz. can corned beef	1/2 tsp. dry mustard
hash	1 8-oz. can tomato sauce
1 8 1/2-oz. can sliced pineapple	

Cook the onions in boiling, salted water for about 20 minutes or until tender. Drain and cool. Slice tops from each onion and lift out centers. Chop centers to make 1/2 cup onion and cook in butter in a saucepan until lightly browned. Add the corned beef hash and stir until well mixed. Fill onions with corned beef mixture and arrange in a baking dish. Drain the pineapple, reserving syrup. Cut pineapple slices in half and place a half slice on top of each stuffed onion. Combine the brown sugar, cornstarch and mustard in a small saucepan. Add reserved pineapple syrup and tomato sauce and cook, stirring constantly, until thickened. Pour over onions. Bake in a 400-degree oven for 20 to 25 minutes. 4-6 servings.

Island-Inspired Onions (above)

CARAMELIZED ONIONS

12 sm. onions, peeled	**Salt and pepper to taste**
1/2 c. brown sugar	**2 tbsp. butter**

Place the onions in a casserole. Mix the brown sugar, salt, pepper, butter and 2 tablespoons hot water and pour over the onions. Bake at 375 degrees for 45 minutes or until done.

Jean Passino, Roanoke, Virginia

MEDITERRANEAN ONIONS

1 lb. small white onions	**1 1/2 tsp. salt**
1/4 c. olive oil	**1 1/2 tsp. salad herbs**
1 1/2 tbsp. wine vinegar	**1/4 c. raisins**

Stick a toothpick crosswise through the center of each onion. Cover the onions with boiling water and add olive oil, vinegar, salt, herbs and raisins. Bring to a boil and simmer for 20 to 25 minutes or until tender but firm. 4-6 servings.

Mrs. Jacob Cozad, Calhoun, Georgia

BAKED ONIONS

6 med.-large onions	**1 tbsp. tomato juice**
1 tbsp. melted butter	**2 tbsp. honey**
1 tsp. salt	**1 tbsp. lemon juice**
1 tsp. paprika	

Peel the onions, and cut in halves crosswise. Place in a buttered casserole. Mix the remaining ingredients and pour over the onions. Cover with foil. Bake at 350 degrees for 1 hour or until tender, basting occasionally.

Mrs. Melvin H. Jones, Granite Falls, North Carolina

CORN-FRIED ONION RINGS

3 lge. white onions	**1 c. self-rising flour**
Milk	**2 c. self-rising cornmeal**
2 eggs, beaten slightly	

Slice the onions, then separate into rings and cover with cold milk. Let stand for 30 minutes in the refrigerator, then drain well, reserving 1/2 cup milk. Mix the eggs with the reserved milk. Dip the onions in the flour, then in the egg mixture. Dip in the cornmeal. Fry in deep 365-degree fat for about 2 minutes or until golden brown and drain on paper towels. Serve hot.

Mrs. Sarah F. Whitehurst, Virginia Beach, Virginia

SMOTHERED LEEKS McLEAN

20 to 24 med.-sized leeks	Dash of thyme
2 tbsp. chopped carrots	1 bay leaf
2 tbsp. minced onions	2 c. beef bouillon
2 tbsp. finely chopped parsley	2 egg yolks, well beaten
2 tbsp. chopped green pepper	1 1/2 c. white sauce
Salt and pepper to taste	1/2 c. buttered bread crumbs
1/4 tsp. nutmeg	

Remove 1 or 2 layers of the white skin from the leeks. Rinse the leeks well and wipe dry. Arrange the leeks in a buttered shallow baking dish. Sprinkle the carrots, onions, parsley and green pepper over the leeks. Add the seasonings and beef bouillon. Cover the baking dish. Bake at 350 degrees for 35 to 40 minutes or until the liquid has been almost absorbed. Combine the egg yolks and white sauce and pour over the leeks. Cover the dish and return to the oven. Bake for 15 to 20 minutes longer or until the sauce is of custard consistency. Remove the cover and sprinkle the bread crumbs over the top. Broil until the crumbs are brown.

Mrs. Patsy McLean, Wolford, Virginia

LEEKS DELIGHT

2 bunches leeks	Salt and pepper to taste
Chicken broth	2 tbsp. butter

Cut the green tops and roots from the leeks. Wash the white bulbs thoroughly. Place the leeks in a saucepan and cover with chicken broth. Bring to a boil and cover. Cook for 15 to 20 minutes or until tender. Season with salt, pepper and butter. 4 servings.

Mrs. Hannah Alford, Heber Springs, Arkansas

ROSEMARY-PARSNIP CASSEROLE

12 parsnips	1/4 c. grated Parmesan cheese
6 tbsp. butter	2 c. half and half
1/4 tsp. rosemary	1/2 c. salted cracker crumbs
2 tbsp. flour	

Peel the parsnips and cook in boiling, salted water for 30 minutes or until tender. Drain and cut in halves lengthwise. Arrange half the parsnips in a greased 2-quart baking dish. Dot with 1 tablespoon butter and sprinkle with half the rosemary, flour and cheese. Drizzle with half the cream. Repeat the layers. Melt the remaining butter and toss with the cracker crumbs. Sprinkle over the top of the casserole. Bake at 400 degrees for 20 minutes. 6 servings.

Marcia E. Nordquist, Greensboro, North Carolina

Oven Pot Roast with Fresh Parsnips (below)

OVEN POT ROAST WITH FRESH PARSNIPS

1 4 to 5-lb. boneless rump,	1/2 c. boiling water
round or chuck beef roast	3 lb. fresh parsnips
2 tbsp. shortening or beef suet	Flour
Salt and pepper	

Preheat oven to 325 degrees. Brown the roast on all sides in shortening, sprinkling with 1 teaspoon salt and 1/4 teaspoon pepper as the roast browns. Place on a rack in a casserole or roaster with tight-fitting lid and pour in the water. Cover. Roast for 1 hour and 15 minutes to 1 hour and 45 minutes. Pare the parsnips and add to roast with 1/2 teaspoon salt. Cover and roast for 45 minutes longer. Place the roast on a warm platter. Surround with parsnips and garnish with fresh parsley. Measure the pan drippings and mix 1 1/2 tablespoons flour with 1 1/2 tablespoons water to a smooth paste for each cup liquid. Return to casserole. Add salt and pepper to taste and cook, stirring, until thickened. 8-10 servings.

PARSNIP BALLS

8 parsnips	1/2 tsp. salt
1/2 c. flour	1/4 tsp. pepper
4 tbsp. melted butter	2 c. fine dry bread crumbs
Milk	3 eggs, beaten

Boil the parsnips in salted water until soft. Cool and remove outer coating and core. Mash the parsnips. Blend the flour with melted butter and add 2 cups milk, salt and pepper gradually. Cook until very thick, stirring constantly, then mix with the parsnips. Refrigerate overnight. Shape into 1-inch balls and roll in the crumbs. Mix the eggs with 2 tablespoons milk, then dip the parsnip balls in the egg mixture. Roll again in crumbs. Fry in deep fat until golden brown.

Kathryn Davis, Nashville, Tennessee

CANDIED PARSNIPS

6 to 8 med.-sized parsnips	1/3 tsp. salt
1/3 c. butter	1 c. brown sugar

Wash and peel the parsnips and cook until tender. Drain and slice lengthwise. Arrange in a shallow pan. Melt the butter in a saucepan and stir in the salt and sugar. Add 1/3 cup water and cook for 5 minutes. Pour the syrup over the parsnips. Bake in 350-degree oven until transparent.

Mrs. W. P. Carter, Boomer, West Virginia

PARSNIPS IN ORANGE SAUCE

12 sm. parsnips, cooked	1/2 tsp. salt
1/2 c. orange juice	1/8 tsp. paprika
2 tbsp. brown sugar	2 tbsp. butter
2 tbsp. light syrup	Grated orange peel

Place the parsnips in a shallow 8 x 12-inch casserole. Combine the orange juice, sugar, syrup, salt and paprika and pour over the parsnips. Dot with butter and sprinkle with orange peel. Bake at 400 degrees for 20 minutes. 6 servings.

Dorothy Williams, Tupelo, Mississippi

GERMAN POTATO SALAD

4 med. potatoes	2/3 c. water
1/4 lb. sliced bacon, diced	1/3 c. vinegar
1/4 c. minced onion	1 egg, slightly beaten
2 tbsp. sugar	3/4 tsp. salt
2 tbsp. flour	

Cook the potatoes in jackets in boiling, salted water until tender. Remove skins and cube potatoes while still as hot as possible. Fry the bacon in a skillet until crisp and remove from skillet. Drain all except 1/4 cup bacon drippings from skillet and return to heat. Add the onion and cook until golden. Add sugar and flour to onion and blend well. Reduce heat and stir in water and vinegar. Add the egg and salt and stir to blend thoroughly. Boil for 1 minute. Add bacon and potatoes and mix gently. Remove from heat and serve hot. 4 servings.

Mrs. George Veith, Louisville, Kentucky

Shoestring Potatoes (page 73); Saratoga Chips, Whole-Browned Potatoes,
French-Fried Potatoes (all below)

FRENCH-FRIED POTATOES

2 1/4 lb. Idaho potatoes   **Salt to taste**
Solid all-vegetable shortening

Pare the potatoes and cut into sticks about 1/4 inch thick. Place potatoes in cold
water as cut. Heat the shortening in a deep fryer to 365 degrees. Drain and dry
potatoes thoroughly. Fry about 1/4 at a time for 10 to 15 minutes or until
golden brown. Drain on paper towels and sprinkle with salt. Keep in warm oven
until all potatoes are fried.

WHOLE-BROWNED POTATOES

2 1/4 lb. small new potatoes   **Salt to taste**
Solid all-vegetable shortening

Pare the potatoes and cook in boiling, salted water until just tender. Drain. Fry in
shortening in deep fryer at 365 degrees for 5 to 10 minutes or until golden
brown. Drain on paper towels and sprinkle with salt. One 2-pound package
frozen whole potatoes, thawed and dried with paper towels, may be substituted
for new potatoes.

SARATOGA CHIPS

2 1/4 lb. Idaho potatoes   **Salt to taste**
Solid all-vegetable shortening

Pare the potatoes and cut into very thin slices with a slicer or sharp knife. Place in cold water as potatoes are sliced. Heat shortening in a deep fryer to 365 degrees. Drain the potatoes and dry thoroughly. Fry about 1/4 of the potatoes at a time in shortening for 5 to 8 minutes or until golden, then drain on paper towels. Sprinkle with salt. Keep in warm oven until all potatoes are fried. 6 servings.

SHOESTRING POTATOES

2 1/4 lb. Idaho potatoes	Salt to taste
Solid all-vegetable shortening	

Pare the potatoes and cut into sticks 1/8 inch thick. Place in cold water as potatoes are cut. Heat shortening in a deep fryer to 365 degrees. Drain the potatoes and dry thoroughly. Fry, 1/4 at a time, in shortening for 8 to 10 minutes or until golden brown, then drain on paper towels. Sprinkle with salt. Keep in warm oven until all potatoes are fried. 6 servings.

BAKED MASHED POTATOES

4 lge. Irish potatoes	1/2 tsp. sage
1/3 c. heavy cream	Salt and pepper to taste
1/2 tsp. rosemary	1/4 c. melted butter
1/2 tsp. minced parsley	Parmesan cheese

Boil the potatoes in the skins, then peel. Mash the potatoes with cream and seasonings. Place in a baking dish and brush with melted butter. Sprinkle with Parmesan cheese. Bake at 450 degrees for 20 minutes.

Mrs. D. F. Donaldson, Savannah, Georgia

VALENTINE PARTY POTATOES

10 med. potatoes, cooked	1 c. sour cream
Milk	1 tsp. garlic salt
1 8-oz. package cream	Butter
cheese	Paprika

Place the potatoes in a mixing bowl and beat with electric mixer until smooth, adding enough milk to moisten. Add the cream cheese, sour cream and garlic salt and beat until mixed. Place in a 2-quart casserole and dot with butter. Sprinkle with paprika. Bake at 350 degrees for 30 minutes. 12 servings.

Mrs. B. A. Stewart, Gadsden, Alabama

BAKED POTATOES WITH CHEF'S SAUCE

5 or 6 baking potatoes	1 c. shredded sharp processed
1/2 c. sour cream	American cheese
1/4 c. soft margarine	2 tbsp. chopped green onion

Scrub the potatoes and wipe dry. Potatoes may be greased before baking for soft skins. Place on baking pan. Bake at 425 degrees for 50 to 60 minutes or until done. Roll gently to make insides mealy; cut across tops. Press ends to fluff. Combine remaining ingredients and spoon over potatoes. 5-6 servings.

Mrs. Ina P. Vance, Atlanta, Georgia

DELUXE AU GRATIN POTATOES

1 onion	4 tbsp. flour
6 sm. potatoes	2 c. milk
Salt	1 c. grated sharp cheese
4 tbsp. margarine	Paprika

Peel and slice the onion and potatoes in a saucepan. Add 2 cups water and bring to a boil. Add 1 teaspoon salt and cover. Cook until tender and drain. Place in a baking dish. Melt the margarine in a saucepan and blend in the flour and 1 teaspoon salt. Add the milk gradually, stirring until smooth. Cook until thickened, stirring constantly. Fold in the cheese and stir until melted. Pour the cheese sauce over the potatoes and sprinkle with paprika. Bake at 400 degrees until bubbly and brown. 6 servings.

Mrs. Oliver Spann, Americus, Georgia

BOILED POTATOES WITH CHEESE SAUCE

10 sm. new potatoes	2 c. milk
1/4 c. margarine	1 c. grated cheese
1/4 c. flour	Salt and pepper to taste

Scrape the potatoes. Cook in boiling, salted water until tender, then drain. Keep warm. Melt the margarine in a saucepan. Add the flour and mix well. Add the milk and cook, stirring constantly, until thickened. Remove from heat. Add the cheese and stir until melted. Stir in the salt and pepper. Place the potatoes in a serving dish and pour the cheese sauce over potatoes.

Photograph for this recipe on page 58.

POTATOES RANCHERO

1/4 c. margarine	3/4 c. chopped green onions
1/4 c. flour	2 c. grated Cheddar cheese
2 c. milk	6 c. sliced cooked potatoes
1 tsp. salt	1 green pepper, cut in rings
1/4 tsp. pepper	1/2 c. barbecue sauce

Melt the margarine in a saucepan, then blend in the flour. Add the milk gradually, stirring until smooth. Add salt and pepper and cook, stirring constantly, until the sauce is thick. Add the onions and cheese and stir until cheese is melted. Alternate layers of potatoes and cheese sauce in 12 x 8-inch baking dish. Top with the green pepper rings and barbecue sauce. Bake at 350 degrees for 25 to 30 minutes. 8 servings.

Judy Hoag, Douglas, Arizona

BERKS COUNTY POTATO DUMPLINGS

6 potatoes	1 onion, grated
10 slices bread	1 tsp. minced parsley
Salt to taste	2 eggs, well beaten
Pepper to taste	Flour

Grate the potatoes. Soak the bread in cold water and squeeze out as much water as possible. Combine the bread, salt, pepper, onion and parsley, then add the potatoes and eggs. Mix well and form into balls. Roll in flour and drop gently into boiling salted water. Cook, covered, for 15 minutes.

Mrs. Myrtle Allanson, Charles City, Virginia

DEEP-DISH CHEESED POTATOES

2 tbsp. butter or margarine	1/8 tsp. seasoned pepper
1/2 c. chopped onion	3/4 c. shredded Cheddar cheese
5 or 6 boiled potatoes	2 eggs, beaten
1 1/2 tsp. seasoned salt	1 c. sour cream

Melt the butter in a skillet. Saute the onion in butter until tender. Peel and slice the potatoes, then place a layer in a well-greased 1 1/2-quart casserole. Mix the onion, salt, pepper and 1/2 cup cheese. Sprinkle over the potato layer. Add another layer of potatoes. Combine the eggs with the sour cream and pour over the potatoes. Sprinkle with remaining cheese. Bake at 375 degrees for 45 minutes. 6 servings.

Mrs. Effie Sullivan, Madison, Tennessee

SCALLOPED POTATOES

4 c. sliced potatoes	1 c. cream
6 tbsp. butter or margarine	1 c. chicken broth
6 tbsp. flour	Salt and pepper to taste
1 c. milk	

Cook the potatoes in boiling, salted water until partially done, then drain. Place in a casserole. Melt the butter in a saucepan. Add the flour and mix well. Add the milk, cream and chicken broth and cook, stirring, until thickened. Add the salt and pepper and pour over potatoes. Bake at 350 degrees for 45 minutes or until brown.

Photograph for this recipe on page 58.

GNOCCHI

1 lb. baking potatoes	1 tbsp. salt
1 1/3 c. all-purpose flour	1 c. coarsely grated Parmesan
1 tsp. salt	cheese
3 qt. boiling water	

Scrub the potatoes and place in a 3-quart saucepan. Cover with cold water and heat to boiling point. Reduce heat and cover. Cook for 25 to 30 minutes or until potatoes are tender. Sift the flour and measure, reserving 2 tablespoons. Drain the potatoes, then peel and put through ricer or food mill. Add the salt and stir in flour gradually. Knead well to form a stiff dough. Divide the dough in half and shape in 2 rolls about 3/4 inch in diameter. Cut rolls in 1-inch lengths. Toss the pieces in the reserved flour. Mark each with tines of a fork making 4 distinct lines. Drop in boiling salted water and boil briskly for about 8 minutes. The Gnocchi will rise to the surface. Drain quickly and arrange in slightly buttered shallow pan. Sprinkle evenly with cheese. Place under broiler 3 inches below heat. Broil until top is browned and crusty. Serve at once. 3 servings.

Donna Umphers, Savannah, Tennessee

HERBED-CREAMED POTATOES

3 c. diced cooked potatoes	1 1/2 tsp. salt
1 c. sour cream	1/2 tsp. ground white pepper
2 tbsp. onion flakes	Paprika
1 tbsp. parsley flakes	

Combine all the ingredients except the paprika in a saucepan. Cook over low heat for 5 minutes or until the cream begins to bubble over the potatoes. Sprinkle with paprika and serve. 4 servings.

Mrs. Jessie Sue Smith, Cullman, Alabama

POTATOES ON THE HALF SHELL

6 med. potatoes	1/4 tsp. pepper
2 tbsp. butter	1/4 c. hot milk
1 tsp. salt	

Place the potatoes on a baking sheet. Bake in 425-degree oven until done. Cut lengthwise into halves. Scoop out the pulp, being careful not to break the shells. Mash thoroughly, then add the butter, salt, pepper and hot milk. Beat until fluffy. Pile the mixture lightly into shells and do not smooth the tops. Return to the oven. Bake until light brown on top. Small bits of pimento, stuffed olives or grated cheese may be sprinkled over top or added to potato mixture. 6-8 servings.

Mrs. Allie Mae Robinson, Henderson, North Carolina

WHIPPED POTATOES PAPRIKA

6 med. potatoes, cubed	Salt and pepper to taste
1 3-oz. package cream cheese	Milk
1/4 c. butter or margarine	Paprika

Cook the potatoes in boiling, salted water until tender, then drain. Add the cream cheese, butter, salt, pepper and enough milk for desired consistency and beat with an electric mixer until smooth and fluffy. Place in a serving dish and sprinkle with paprika.

Photograph for this recipe on page 58.

CRUNCHY BAKED POTATOES

1/3 c. instant nonfat dry milk	Dash of cayenne pepper
1/3 c. water	6 baked potato shells
2 c. mashed potatoes	1 c. crumbled corn flakes
1/4 c. finely chopped onion	1/2 c. grated Parmesan cheese
1 egg, well beaten	3 tbsp. melted butter
1 tsp. salt	

Whip the milk and water until thick and smooth. Mix in the potatoes, onion, egg, salt and cayenne pepper and beat until light and fluffy. Place in the baked potato shells. Place shells in a baking dish. Mix the corn flakes, Parmesan cheese and butter and sprinkle over potato mixture. Bake in 375-degree oven for 20 to 25 minutes. This recipe may be used in preparing potato casserole or potato puffs. 6 servings.

Crunchy Baked Potatoes (above)

HASHED BROWN POTATOES

3 c. cubed cooked potatoes
1 tsp. salt
1/8 tsp. pepper

1 tbsp. minced onion
1/4 c. margarine

Sprinkle the potatoes with salt, pepper and onion. Heat the margarine in a skillet. Add the potatoes and cook until brown, stirring frequently. Place in a serving dish and garnish with parsley.

Photograph for this recipe on page 58.

DELUXE POTATO-EGG CASSEROLE

1 4-oz. can mushrooms,
    drained
1/4 c. butter or margarine
1/4 c. flour
1 tsp. onion salt
1 tsp. celery salt
3/4 tsp. salt

1/4 tsp. pepper
3 c. milk
1 1-lb. package frozen
    French fries
1/4 lb. Cheddar cheese, cubed
8 hard-cooked eggs, chopped

Cook the mushrooms in butter in a saucepan for 5 minutes and blend in flour and seasonings. Add milk all at once and cook, stirring constantly, until thickened. Stir in French fries and cheese and pour half the mixture into a greased 2-quart baking dish. Top with eggs and add remaining potato mixture. Bake at 400 degrees for 20 minutes or until bubbly and golden brown. 6 servings.

Mrs. Louis Christensen, Cullman, Alabama

POTATO SALAD

4 med. potatoes, cooked
2 hard-cooked eggs, chopped
3 tbsp. chopped pimento
3 tbsp. chopped celery
3 tbsp. chopped pickle

2 tbsp. finely chopped onion
1 tsp. salt
1/3 to 1/2 c. mayonnaise
Salad greens

Peel the potatoes and cut in cubes. Combine with the eggs, pimento, celery, pickle, onion, salt and mayonnaise and chill. Serve on salad greens. 6 servings.

Mrs. Willie Vee Hill, Philadelphia, Mississippi

CREAMED RADISHES

4 pkg. fresh radishes
2 tbsp. flour
1 c. milk

1/8 tsp. curry powder
1 tbsp. margarine

Pare and cut off the ends of the radishes. Cover the radishes halfway with cold water in a saucepan. Cover and cook for 10 minutes, then remove from heat. Make a paste with the flour and 2 tablespoons milk. Stir in the remaining milk until smooth. Add the milk mixture to the hot liquid in the saucepan. Stir and add curry powder, blending well. Cook until the sauce is smooth. Add the margarine and serve. 4 servings.

Mrs. Glenn Marshall, Shreveport, Louisiana

RUTABAGA CASSEROLE

1 med. rutabaga	White pepper to taste
2 tbsp. butter	1 tbsp. brown sugar or syrup
2 tbsp. toast crumbs	Salt to taste
1/2 c. milk	Nutmeg to taste
1 egg	

Peel, rinse and slice the rutabaga. Cook until soft and mash. Mix in the butter and 1 tablespoon crumbs. Combine the milk and egg in a bowl and beat well. Add the beaten mixture, white pepper, sugar, salt and nutmeg to the rutabaga mixture. Pour into well-greased mold or casserole and sprinkle remaining crumbs and additional nutmeg on top. Bake at 350 degrees for 30 minutes. 6-8 servings.

Mrs. Alison Duke, Chattanooga, Tennessee

MASHED RUTABAGA

1 lge. rutabaga	2 tbsp. butter
1 tsp. salt	1/4 c. heavy cream
Pepper to taste	

Peel the rutabaga and cut into slices or cubes. Cook in boiling, salted water for 15 to 20 minutes or until tender and drain thoroughly. Mash fine with potato masher and season. Add the butter and cream. Heat and serve. 6 servings.

Mrs. Audra Reich, Miami, Florida

RUTABAGA-APPLE BLEND

4 rutabagas	2 tbsp. butter
2 apples	Salt and pepper to taste

Peel the rutabagas and cut in slices into a saucepan. Add a small amount of water and bring to a boil. Cover and cook until tender, then drain and mash. Peel and quarter the apples. Place in a saucepan in a small amount of water and cook until tender. Mash or sieve the apples until smooth. Combine the mashed rutabagas and the apple puree and add the butter. Season with the salt and pepper and serve.

Mrs. Anna Keen, Wilmington, Delaware

CANDIED SWEET POTATOES

2 lge. sweet potatoes	1/2 c. brown sugar
1/2 c. melted butter	1/2 tsp. cinnamon
1/2 c. sugar	1/4 tsp. ginger

Quarter the sweet potatoes and place in a saucepan. Cover with water and bring to a boil. Cook until tender and drain. Arrange in a buttered baking dish. Combine and add the remaining ingredients. Bake at 300 degrees for 20 minutes.

Jewel Hardcastle, Clarksville, Arkansas

SWEET POTATO PUDDING OF 1828

1 lb. cooked and peeled sweet potatoes	1 tbsp. grated lemon rind
1 1/4 c. sugar	1/4 tsp. mace
1/2 c. margarine, melted	1 c. orange juice
6 egg yolks, well beaten	6 egg whites
	1 tbsp. slivered citron

Rub the sweet potatoes through a sieve, then add 1 cup sugar and margarine. Combine with the egg yolks, lemon rind, mace and orange juice. Beat the egg whites until stiff, then fold carefully into sweet potato mixture. Place in a well-greased 3-quart baking dish. Sprinkle with the remaining sugar and slivered citron. Bake in 350-degree oven for about 1 hour. 8-10 servings.

Mrs. Richard A. Shell, Emporia, Virginia

YAM-BANANA CASSEROLE

2 lge. sweet potatoes	3/4 c. (packed) brown sugar
Juice of 1 lemon	1/4 c. butter
2 bananas, sliced crosswise	

Cook the sweet potatoes in boiling water until tender. Peel and slice crosswise. Pour lemon juice over bananas. Place alternate layers of sweet potatoes and bananas in a greased casserole, sprinkling each layer with sugar. Dot with butter. Bake at 350 degrees for 25 minutes or until lightly browned. 4-6 servings.

Mrs. Herbert H. Bidwell, Lubbock, Texas

SWEET POTATO-NUT LOGS

1 1-lb. can sweet potatoes, drained	1 tsp. salt
1/4 c. butter, melted	1/2 c. nuts

Drain the sweet potatoes, then mash in a large mixing bowl. Blend in the butter and salt. Form into 6 to 8 small logs and roll in the nuts. Place in a greased shallow pan. Bake at 325 degrees for 30 to 45 minutes.

Mrs. Fred R. Smith, Pilot Mt., North Carolina

LEMON-SWEET POTATOES

6 baking-sized potatoes	1 stick margarine
1 c. brown sugar	1/2 lemon, sliced
1 c. sugar	1 tsp. vanilla

Bake the sweet potatoes at 350 degrees for about 1 hour or until done. Peel and cut in half lengthwise. Combine the sugars, margarine and lemon slices in a saucepan. Cook until light syrup forms, then add the potatoes. Cook until syrup thickens. Cool and add vanilla.

Mrs. W. K. Parkman, Prentiss, Mississippi

HOT LOUISIANA YAM SALAD

10 slices bacon	1/4 tsp. freshly ground pepper
3 sm. onions, thinly sliced	1/4 tsp. ground cinnamon
1 1/2 c. sliced celery	Dash of ground ginger
1/4 c. vinegar	3 16-oz. cans Louisiana
2 tsp. (firmly packed) light	yams
brown sugar	1/4 c. chopped parsley
1/2 tsp. salt	

Cook the bacon in a skillet until crisp, then drain on paper towels. Crumble. Pour off all except 1/4 cup drippings from skillet. Add the onions and celery and cook until tender, stirring occasionally. Stir in the vinegar, brown sugar, salt, pepper, cinnamon and ginger and bring to a boil, stirring constantly. Remove from heat. Place the yams and liquid in a saucepan and cover. Heat for about 5 minutes, then drain well. Toss yams with onion mixture, parsley and bacon and serve warm. 6 servings.

Hot Louisiana Yam Salad (above)

Savory Mashed Louisiana Yams with Apples (below)

SAVORY MASHED LOUISIANA YAMS WITH APPLES

4 med. cooked Louisiana yams, peeled	Dash of onion salt
6 tbsp. butter or margarine	1/8 tsp. ground thyme
2 tbsp. chopped parsley	Pepper to taste
3/4 tsp. salt	1 tbsp. lemon juice
	1 med. tart apple

Mash the yams with 4 tablespoons butter, parsley, seasonings and lemon juice. Turn into a 9-inch pie plate and spread evenly. Cut the apple in thin wedges and cook in remaining butter in a saucepan for 1 minute. Arrange apple wedges on yam mixture and pour butter from the saucepan over yam mixture. Bake in 375-degree oven for 15 minutes. Serve with baked ham, if desired. Two 16-ounce cans Louisiana yams, drained, may be substituted for fresh yams. 4 servings.

PRIZE SWEET POTATO-PECAN PIE

1 1/2 c. mashed sweet potatoes	2 well-beaten eggs
1 c. brown sugar	1 9-in. unbaked pie shell
1 tsp. cinnamon	1/4 c. butter
1 tsp. ginger	3/4 c. broken pecan meats
1/2 tsp. salt	Whipped cream
1 1/2 c. scalded milk	

Combine the potatoes with 1/2 cup brown sugar, cinnamon, ginger, salt, milk and eggs and cool. Pour in a pie shell. Bake in a 350-degree oven for about 20 minutes or until nearly set. Mix the butter, remaining sugar and pecans and sprinkle over top of pie. Bake for about 45 minutes longer or until custard is done. Serve with whipped cream, if desired.

Ona M. Warren, Jewett, Texas

TOP-OF-THE-STOVE TURNIPS

1 c. water	1/2 c. sliced onion
1 c. milk	1/4 c. diced celery
1 tsp. salt	1/4 c. diced green pepper
3 c. pared thinly sliced white	1 tbsp. butter or margarine
turnips	1 c. grated American cheese
2 c. pared sliced carrots	3 tbsp. finely crumbled crackers

Bring the water and milk to a boil in a heatproof casserole, then add the salt, turnips, carrots, onion, celery and green pepper. Simmer, covered, for about 20 minutes or until tender. Add the butter, cheese and cracker crumbs. Heat, covered, until the cheese is melted. 6 servings.

Augusta Jannett, Yoakum, Texas

GARDEN PATCH TURNIPS

1 lb. turnips	1/3 c. cream
4 tbsp. butter, melted	Salt and pepper to taste
4 tbsp. flour	3 eggs, separated
1 tbsp. onion, minced	

Wash, pare and slice the turnips. Cook in boiling salted water for about 3 minutes. Drain and mash, reserving 1/3 cup liquid. Blend the butter and flour in a saucepan. Add the onion, reserved liquid and cream. Add the mashed turnips and seasonings, then add to well-beaten egg yolks, stirring constantly. Fold in stiffly beaten egg whites and pour into a buttered baking dish. Cover. Bake at 350 degrees for about 30 minutes. 6 servings.

Mrs. Herbert H. Jeffers, Oneida, Tennessee

KOHLRABI IN SAUCE

6 med. kohlrabi bulbs	3 tbsp. flour
Kohlrabi leaves	1/2 c. milk
2 tbsp. butter or margarine	Salt and pepper to taste

Peel and cube the kohlrabi bulbs. Cook in boiling, salted water for 15 to 20 minutes. Cook the fresh, green leaves in boiling salted water for 20 minutes. Drain the cubes, reserving 1/2 cup liquid. Drain the greens and chop coarsely. Melt the butter in a saucepan. Add the flour, stirring until smooth. Pour the reserved liquid and milk gradually into the flour mixture, stirring constantly. Cook until thickened and add the kohlrabi cubes and leaves. Season with salt and pepper.

Mrs. Marie Huffstutler, Searcy, Arkansas

Party Broccoli (page 93)

stalk vegetables

The vegetables included in this group are some of the best-loved southern favorites — tender asparagus, a treat by itself or with a rich Hollandaise sauce . . . crunchy bamboo shoots, adding an exotic note to every meal . . . crisp celery . . . rich cauliflower . . . broccoli, and more.

Women who cook to please their families and friends — southern women — have taken these favorite vegetables and used them as the basis of rich and flavorful dishes. Now, in the section that follows, you can discover dozens of these recipes which are certain to become favorites with your family, too.

In Vegetables Chop Suey, vegetables are cooked to the peak of their taste in the oriental manner. Feature this dish with fried rice and perhaps sweet and sour pork — it will bring warm compliments from your happy family! For that extra-special dinner or party, serve Cauliflower with Dill Sauce or Broccoli with Bleu Cheese. These two recipes combine the full flavor of stalk vegetables with highly-seasoned sauces . . . and delight everyone's palate! Is asparagus one of your family's favorites? Highlight it in Tasty April Asparagus and watch it become the center of attraction!

These are just some of the innovative, family-approved recipes awaiting you in these pages. Serve a stalk vegetable dish tonight — and bring new flavor excitement to your dinner table!

85

Salmon Suey (below)

SALMON SUEY

1 1-lb. can salmon	1 tbsp. cornstarch
2 tbsp. oil	1/4 c. water
1/2 c. chopped onion	1 c. sliced bamboo shoots
1/2 c. chopped celery	1/4 c. sliced water
1/2 tsp. salt	chestnuts (opt.)
1/4 tsp. pepper	1 1-lb. can bean sprouts,
1 tsp. sugar	drained
Soy sauce to taste	1 1-lb. can Chinese noodles
1/2 green pepper, cut into	or cooked rice
thin strips	

Drain the salmon and reserve liquid. Heat the oil in a skillet. Add the onion and celery and saute for 5 minutes or until onion is golden. Add reserved salmon liquid, salt, pepper, sugar, soy sauce and green pepper and cover. Simmer for 10 minutes. Blend the cornstarch with water and stir into onion mixture. Cook over low heat, stirring, until slightly thickened. Stir in the bamboo shoots, water chestnuts and bean sprouts. Remove bones from salmon and flake the salmon. Add to the skillet and cover. Simmer for 5 minutes longer. Serve with Chinese noodles. 4 servings.

BAMBOO SHOOTS

Young tender bamboo shoots   **Water**

Place bamboo shoots in water to cover in saucepan. Boil for 10 to 15 minutes and discard the water. Bamboo shoots are a delicate accompaniment for meat or a crisp ingredient in chop suey and chow mein dishes.

Mrs. Ernest Chandler, Baton Rouge, Louisiana

VEGETABLE CHOP SUEY

1 c. canned bean sprouts	3 tbsp. soy sauce
1/4 c. sliced bamboo shoots	1/2 tsp. monosodium glutamate
1/4 c. sliced canned mushrooms	1/2 tsp. sugar
1 c. shredded cabbage	Salt to taste
1/4 c. sliced celery	1/4 c. soup stock or water
1/2 c. green peas	1 tbsp. cornstarch
4 tbsp. salad oil	1/2 c. water

Drain the bean sprouts. Combine the vegetables and fry in hot oil in a skillet over high heat for 2 to 3 minutes. Add the seasonings and soup stock. Cover and simmer over moderate heat for 6 to 8 minutes. Mix the cornstarch and water together and stir into the vegetable mixture. Cook for 5 minutes or until the sauce thickens. 4 servings.

Mrs. Eunice Swift, Las Cruces, New Mexico

CAULIFLOWER-SPAGHETTI CASSEROLE

1 med. cauliflower	1 1/2 c. cooked spaghetti
2 c. canned tomatoes	1/2 c. buttered bread crumbs
Salt and pepper	1/2 c. grated cheese
3 tbsp. melted butter	

Cook the cauliflower in salted water to cover until tender and drain. Break the cauliflower into flowerets. Heat the tomatoes over hot water and season to taste. Add the butter. Arrange alternate layers of cauliflower and spaghetti in a well-oiled casserole. Add the tomatoes and cover with bread crumbs. Sprinkle the cheese over all. Bake at 350 degrees for 30 minutes. 6 servings.

Corinne R. Davison, Prescott, Arkansas

CAULIFLOWER SOUFFLE

1 lge. cauliflower	3 eggs, separated
1/3 c. butter	3 tbsp. grated Parmesan cheese
2 tbsp. flour	Seasonings to taste
1 c. milk	

Boil the cauliflower until tender in salted water. Separate into flowerets and remove most of the stem. Place the cauliflower in a baking dish. Melt the butter in a saucepan and blend in the flour and milk gradually. Cook, stirring constantly, until thickened. Remove from heat and add the egg yolks. Cool and fold in stiffly beaten egg whites and cheese. Season and pour over the cauliflower. Bake at 350 degrees for 30 to 45 minutes. 4-6 servings.

Mrs. Dorothy Smith, Palacios, Texas

Fresh Cauliflower-Tomato Scallop (below)

FRESH CAULIFLOWER-TOMATO SCALLOP

1 lge. head fresh cauliflower	1/4 tsp. pepper
5 tbsp. butter or margarine	1/4 c. flour
1/2 c. finely chopped fresh celery	2 c. milk
1/4 c. finely chopped fresh onion	1 1/2 c. shredded sharp Cheddar cheese
1/4 c. finely chopped fresh green pepper	3 lge. firm ripe fresh tomatoes, sliced
3/4 tsp. salt	1/2 c. soft bread crumbs

Preheat oven to 400 degrees. Separate the cauliflower into flowerets. Cook, covered, in 1 inch boiling, salted water for about 5 minutes or until crisp-tender, lifting cover occasionally to allow steam to escape. Drain. Melt the butter in a saucepan. Add the celery, onion and green pepper and saute until onion is limp and transparent. Blend in the salt, pepper and flour. Add the milk and cook over low heat, stirring constantly, until thickened. Add cheese and stir until heated. Remove from heat. Arrange half the cauliflower in a shallow baking dish or casserole and top with 1/3 of the cheese sauce. Cover with sliced tomatoes and half the remaining sauce. Top with remaining cauliflower and sauce and sprinkle with bread crumbs. Bake for 25 minutes or until brown. 6 servings.

CAULIFLOWER WITH DILL SAUCE

1 med. cauliflower	1 c. sour cream
2 tbsp. butter	1 tsp. dillseed

Separate the cauliflower into flowerets. Place in a pan with a small amount of boiling water. Cover and bring to a boil. Reduce heat and cook until tender but crisp. Melt the butter and add the sour cream and dillseed. Cook until hot but do not boil. Add to the cauliflower just before serving. 6 servings.

Carolyn Carpenter, Arlington, Texas

CAULIFLOWER-OLIVE SALAD

1/2 c. olive oil	1/2 sm. head cauliflower
1/4 c. lemon juice	1/2 c. sliced stuffed olives
1/2 tsp. salt	1 med. head iceberg lettuce
Dash of pepper	1/2 c. crumbled blue cheese
2 Bermuda onions	

Combine the oil, lemon juice, salt and pepper. Slice the onions and separate in rings. Slice the cauliflower. Add the onions, cauliflower and olives to the oil mixture and marinate for at least 30 minutes. Tear the lettuce in small pieces into a salad bowl. Sprinkle the cheese over the lettuce. Add the marinated mixture and toss gently. 6 servings.

Janice Thomas, Auburn, Alabama

FRENCH-FRIED CAULIFLOWER

1 pkg. frozen cauliflower	1 egg
1 tsp. salt	1 c. cracker crumbs
1/4 c. milk	

Prepare the cauliflower according to package directions and drain. Season with salt. Blend the milk with the egg, then dip the cauliflower into the egg mixture. Roll in the cracker crumbs. Drop into hot fat and cook until golden brown. 3-4 servings.

Mrs. Donna Johns, Augusta, Georgia

CAULIFLOWER AU GRATIN

1 head cauliflower	1 tsp. mustard
Salt to taste	Juice of 1/2 lemon
Butter	Ground pepper to taste
1/2 c. flour	4 tbsp. whipped cream
2 1/2 c. hot milk	4 tbsp. fresh bread crumbs
1 1/2 c. grated Gruyere cheese	

Remove the outer green leaves, then wash the cauliflower and leave in cold water for 30 minutes. Cut the cauliflower into flowerets. Cook in salted water for 20 minutes or until tender and drain. Melt 1/2 cup butter in the top of a double boiler. Blend in the flour and cook over hot water, stirring constantly until smooth. Add the hot milk gradually and cook, stirring constantly, until sauce comes to a boil. Add the cheese and cook, stirring until cheese melts. Season with the mustard, lemon juice, salt and pepper. Place the cauliflower in a buttered baking dish and pour the cheese sauce over the cauliflower. Spread with whipped cream and sprinkle with the bread crumbs. Dot with butter. Bake at 375 degrees for about 20 minutes or until top is golden. 4 servings.

Mrs. John F. Jackson, Jr., Wheeling, West Virginia

CAULIFLOWER CASSEROLE

1 lge. head cauliflower	1 tbsp. salt
1/4 c. green pepper, chopped	1 6-oz. can mushrooms
1/4 c. margarine	6 slices pimento cheese
1/4 c. flour	Cracker crumbs
2 c. milk	

Cook the cauliflower for 15 minutes and drain. Saute the pepper in margarine and add flour gradually. Add the milk and salt. Cook over low heat, stirring constantly until thick. Drain the mushrooms and add to the sauce. Alternate layers of cauliflower, cheese and sauce in a baking dish. Cover with cracker crumbs. Bake in 350-degree oven for 15 minutes or until browned and bubbly.

Mrs. Karl Augustin, Loretto, Tennessee

CAULIFLOWER AND ONION FROMAGE

1 med. cauliflower	1/8 tsp. pepper
2 tsp. salt	1 1/4 c. milk
1 No. 2 can sm. onions	1/4 lb. grated sharp cheese
1/2 stick margarine	1 tsp. Worcestershire sauce
1/4 c. flour	

Break the cauliflower into flowerets and soak in cold water for 1 hour before cooking. Cover with water and 1 teaspoon salt and boil for about 10 minutes or until slightly tender. Drain. Place a layer of cauliflower in a 1 1/2-quart casserole, then a layer of onions. Melt the margarine and add the flour, blending well. Add remaining salt and pepper and add the milk, stirring constantly. Stir in the cheese and Worcestershire sauce and pour over layers of onion and cauliflower. Bake for 30 to 40 minutes in a 350-degree oven.

Sue Jones, Flora, Mississippi

CAULIFLOWER WITH TOMATO-CHEESE SAUCE

1 med. cauliflower	1/2 c. grated cheese
Salt	1 tbsp. lemon juice
2 tbsp. flour	Buttered bread crumbs
1 c. tomato juice	

Remove the leaves and stalk from the cauliflower and separate flowerets. Place upside down in water and add 1 tablespoon salt per quart of water. Let stand for 30 minutes and drain. Rinse in cold water, then cover with boiling water. Boil until the cauliflower is tender and drain. Place the cauliflower in a well-oiled baking dish. Mix flour to a smooth paste with a small amount of the tomato juice. Add remaining juice and season. Cook over hot water until thickened, then add the cheese and lemon juice. Pour over the cauliflower. Cover with buttered crumbs. Bake at 400 degrees until brown. 6 servings.

Mrs. Rebecca B. Johnson, Chattanooga, Tennessee

CAULIFLOWER MOLD

2 eggs	1/2 c. soft bread crumbs
1 can cream of celery soup	2 pimentos, chopped
1/2 c. grated cheese	2 tbsp. chopped onion
1 lge. cauliflower, coarsely	1 tsp. salt
chopped	1/8 tsp. pepper

Beat the eggs slightly in a large bowl, then stir in all remaining ingredients. Pour into a buttered casserole. Set in a pan of hot water. Bake at 375 degrees for 50 minutes or until firm. Serve hot. 4-6 servings.

Voncile Owens, Natchitoches, Louisiana

SOUTH AFRICAN ROCK LOBSTER OVER CAULIFLOWER

6 4-oz. frozen South African	3 tbsp. flour
rock lobster-tails	White pepper to taste
1 med. head cauliflower	1/2 tsp. paprika
Salt to taste	1 c. milk
3 tbsp. butter	

Place the lobster-tails in boiling, salted water and cook for 5 minutes. Drain immediately and reserve 1 cup liquid. Drench lobster-tails with cold water. Remove lobster from shells and cut into bite-sized pieces. Wash the cauliflower in cold water, then place in a saucepan with enough cold water to cover. Add the salt and bring to a boil. Reduce heat and cook for 15 minutes. Drain. Melt the butter in a saucepan. Add the flour and mix well. Add the seasonings, milk and reserved lobster liquid and cook, stirring constantly, until thickened. Add the lobster and heat through. Place the cauliflower in a serving bowl and pour lobster mixture over cauliflower. Serve immediately. 6 servings.

South African Rock Lobster Over Cauliflower (above)

Broccoli Spoon Bread (below)

BROCCOLI SPOON BREAD

1 bunch broccoli	**2 tsp. baking powder**
1/2 c. yellow cornmeal	**1 tsp. salt**
1 1/2 c. milk	**1 tbsp. sugar**
2 eggs, separated	

Cut off large leaves and the bottom of the stalks of broccoli. Wash well. Make 2 lengthwise slits almost to the flowerets if stalks are more than 1/2 inch in diameter. Cook the broccoli, uncovered, in boiling, salted water to cover for about 15 minutes or until tender. Drain and reserve 1/2 cup liquid. Place the cornmeal in a medium saucepan and stir in milk gradually. Cook over medium heat, stirring constantly, for about 5 minutes or until thickened. Remove from heat and cool slightly. Beat the egg yolks until well mixed. Add to the cornmeal mixture along with baking powder, salt and sugar and mix well. Beat the egg whites until stiff but not dry, then fold into cornmeal mixture. Arrange the broccoli, stems to center, in a well-greased 1 1/2-quart casserole or baking dish. Pour cornmeal mixture over broccoli and smooth over the broccoli and to the edge of the casserole. Bake in 375-degree oven for 45 to 50 minutes or until golden brown.

Parmesan Sauce

2 tbsp. butter or margarine	**1 c. milk**
1 tbsp. cornstarch	**1 c. grated Parmesan cheese**

1/2 tsp. salt	1/4 tsp. nutmeg
1/8 tsp. white pepper	

Melt the butter in a small saucepan. Stir in the cornstarch until smooth, then stir in milk gradually. Place over low heat and cook, stirring constantly, until mixture comes to a boil. Cook for 3 minutes longer, stirring. Add the cheese, small amount at a time, and stir until melted. Stir in reserved broccoli liquid, salt, pepper and nutmeg and heat through. Serve with the bread.

PARTY BROCCOLI

2 pkg. frozen broccoli	1/2 tsp. poppy seed
2 tbsp. butter	1/2 tsp. paprika
2 tbsp. minced onion	1/4 tsp. salt
1 1/2 c. sour cream	Dash of cayenne pepper
2 tsp. sugar	1/3 c. chopped cashews
1 tsp. white vinegar	

Cook the broccoli according to package directions until just tender, then drain. Melt the butter in a small saucepan. Add the onion and saute until tender. Remove from heat and stir in the sour cream, sugar, vinegar, poppy seed, paprika, salt and cayenne pepper. Arrange the broccoli on a heated platter and pour sour cream sauce over broccoli. Sprinkle with cashews. 6-8 servings.

Photograph for this recipe on page 84.

BROCCOLI CASSEROLE WITH COTTAGE CHEESE

1 sm. carton cottage cheese	3 eggs, beaten
1 pkg. chopped frozen broccoli, thawed	1/4 c. soft butter or margarine
1/4 lb. cheese, diced	3 tbsp. flour
	Salt and pepper to taste

Combine all the ingredients well and place in a buttered 2-quart casserole. Bake, covered, at 350 degrees for 1 hour or until done. 4 servings.

Caroline J. Ebell, Yuma, Arizona

ITALIAN-STYLE BROCCOLI

1/4 c. tomato sauce	1/4 tsp. oregano
2 tbsp. butter	2 lb. fresh broccoli, cooked
1 tbsp. vinegar	1/2 c. grated Parmesan cheese

Combine the tomato sauce, butter, vinegar and oregano in a saucepan and heat. Drain the broccoli and place in a serving dish. Pour the sauce over the broccoli, then sprinkle with the cheese. Serve immediately. 8 servings.

Rose Marie Tondl, Mesa, Arizona

BROCCOLI AND HAM CASSEROLE

12 slices bread
3/4 lb. sharp cheese slices
1 10-oz. package frozen broccoli, cooked
2 c. diced cooked ham

6 eggs, slightly beaten
3 1/2 c. milk
2 tbsp. dried minced onion
1/2 tsp. salt
1/4 tsp. dry mustard

Cut the bread into doughnuts and holes with doughnut cutter. Tear the remaining bread scraps into small pieces and place in 13 x 9 x 2-inch pan. Layer the cheese, broccoli and ham over the bread and top with doughnuts and holes. Combine the remaining ingredients and pour over layers. Cover and refrigerate for 6 hours or overnight. Bake, uncovered, at 325 degrees for 55 minutes. 12 servings.

Mrs. Alice Todd, Miami, Florida

BROCCOLI AND MACARONI HOLLANDAISE

3 tbsp. butter
3 tbsp. flour
1 1/2 tsp. salt
1/8 tsp. pepper
1 1/2 c. milk

3/4 c. mayonnaise
1 7-oz. package macaroni
2 c. cooked chopped broccoli
1 c. grated yellow cheese

Melt the butter and stir in the flour, salt and pepper. Add the milk gradually and cook, stirring constantly, until thickened. Fold in the mayonnaise. Cook the macaroni in boiling salted water until tender. Drain and rinse, then drain again. Place layers of macaroni, broccoli and sauce in a greased 1 1/2-quart casserole, ending with sauce. Sprinkle with the cheese. Bake at 350 degrees for 20 minutes. 4-6 servings.

Mrs. Leon F. Steinle, Jourdanton, Texas

BROCCOLI CASSEROLE

2 10-oz. packages frozen broccoli
1/4 c. minced onion
6 tbsp. butter
5 tbsp. flour
1 tsp. dry mustard
3/4 tsp. salt
1/8 tsp. marjoram
1/8 tsp. monosodium glutamate

3 dashes of hot pepper sauce
3 1/2 c. milk
2 chicken bouillon cubes
5 egg yolks, beaten
1 1/2 c. grated sharp cheese
1 4-oz. can mushrooms
3 tbsp. slivered almonds
Dash of paprika

Cook broccoli until tender and drain. Arrange in a shallow baking dish. Saute the onion in butter, then blend in the flour and seasonings. Add the milk and bouillon cubes and simmer until thickened. Add a small amount of hot sauce to the egg yolks, then stir into remaining hot sauce. Add the cheese and stir until melted. Add the mushrooms. Pour the sauce over the broccoli and sprinkle with almonds and paprika. Bake at 350 degrees for 20 minutes. 6-8 servings.

Mrs. C. E. Stevenson, Alum Ridge, Virginia

BROCCOLI LOAF

1 tbsp. butter	1 c. cream
1 tbsp. flour	1 c. mayonnaise
1/2 tsp. salt	2 c. chopped cooked broccoli
3 eggs, beaten	

Melt the butter in a saucepan, then stir in the flour and salt. Mix the eggs, cream and mayonnaise well and stir into the flour mixture. Combine the sauce and the broccoli and pour into a loaf pan. Set in a pan of water. Bake at 350 degrees for 30 minutes. 8 servings.

Mary Mathis, Lubbock, Texas

BROCCOLI WITH BLEU CHEESE

2 pkg. frozen broccoli	1 tbsp. sugar
3 tbsp. oil	2 oz. bleu cheese, crumbled
2 tbsp. vinegar	Paprika

Cook the broccoli according to package directions and drain. Place the broccoli in a serving dish. Combine the oil, vinegar and sugar in a small saucepan and bring to a boil. Remove from heat and add the cheese. Pour over the broccoli and sprinkle with paprika. 8 servings.

Mrs. Elizabeth W. Knape, Douglas, Arizona

BROCCOLI SALAD MOLD

1 pkg. frozen broccoli	Dash of hot sauce
3 hard-boiled eggs, chopped	2 env. unflavored gelatin
2 tsp. lemon juice	1 can beef consomme
1 1/2 tsp. salt	3/4 c. mayonnaise
4 tsp. Worcestershire sauce	

Cook the broccoli in small amount of water in a saucepan until tender, then drain. Mash and mix with eggs, lemon juice, salt, Worcestershire sauce and hot sauce. Soften the gelatin in small amount of consomme in a saucepan. Add remaining consomme and heat until gelatin is dissolved. Cool. Add the broccoli mixture and mayonnaise and pour into a greased mold. Chill until firm. Serve on lettuce and garnish with French dressing.

Mrs. Jack B. Smith, Bradenton, Florida

TART RHUBARB SALAD

4 c. diced fresh rhubarb	1 3-oz. package strawberry
1 c. water	gelatin
3/4 c. sugar	2 tbsp. lemon juice
1/4 tsp. salt	1 11-oz. can mandarin oranges

Combine the rhubarb, 1 cup water, sugar and salt in a saucepan and bring to a boil. Reduce heat and simmer just until the rhubarb loses crispness. Remove from heat and add gelatin. Stir until dissolved and add the lemon juice. Drain the oranges, reserving the juice. Add enough water to the reserved juice to make 1 cup liquid and stir into the rhubarb mixture. Chill until partially thickened, then fold in the oranges. Spoon into an 8-inch square glass dish and chill until firm. 8 servings.

Mrs. S. R. Spratling, Augusta, Georgia

RHUBARB CRUNCH

1 c. sifted flour	4 c. cut rhubarb
3/4 c. oats	1 c. sugar
1 c. (firmly packed) brown sugar	2 tbsp. cornstarch
1/2 c. melted butter	1 c. water
1 tsp. cinnamon	1 tsp. lemon flavoring

Combine the flour, oats, brown sugar, butter and cinnamon. Place half the crumb mixture in a 9-inch square pan. Add the rhubarb. Combine sugar, cornstarch, water and flavoring in a saucepan and cook until thick and clear. Pour over rhubarb and cover with remaining crumb mixture. Bake at 350 degrees for 1 hour. Serve warm or cold with cream. 9 servings.

Jane Perkins, Richmond, Virginia

ASPARAGUS TIPS

1 lb. asparagus tips	1/2 stick margarine
1/2 tsp. salt	Pepper to taste

Cook the asparagus in salted water for 20 minutes or until tender, then drain. Add the margarine, stirring until melted. Sprinkle with pepper. 6 servings.

Mrs. Earl L. Wilborn, Section, Alabama

TASTY APRIL ASPARAGUS

2 pkg. frozen asparagus	1/2 tsp. thyme
2 green onions, chopped	1/3 c. red wine
6 stuffed olives, chopped	1/4 c. wine vinegar
1 tbsp. capers	3/4 c. olive oil
1 tsp. salt	1/2 tsp. pepper

Cook the asparagus according to package directions and drain. Combine the remaining ingredients and pour over warm asparagus. Turn the asparagus with forks to coat with dressing. Let stand for several hours. 6-8 servings.

Denise L. Hodnette, Pensacola, Florida

BAKED ASPARAGUS SUPREME

1 lb. fresh asparagus
2 c. bread cubes
4 tbsp. butter or margarine
5 hard-boiled eggs, chopped

1 1/2 c. half and half
4 tbsp. flour
Salt and pepper to taste

Cut the asparagus in small pieces and cook in boiling, salted water until tender. Drain. Brown the bread cubes lightly in butter in a skillet. Place half the bread cubes in a greased 2-quart casserole and add half the asparagus. Add half the eggs, then add remaining asparagus. Add remaining eggs and place remaining bread cubes on top. Add the half and half to the flour gradually and add salt and pepper. Pour over casserole. Bake at 350 degrees for 45 minutes. 8-10 servings.

Mrs. Ralph Heatwole, Dayton, Virginia

STEAMED FRESH ASPARAGUS

1 lb. fresh asparagus   1/4 c. melted butter

Leave the asparagus whole or cut into 2-inch lengths. Place the asparagus in a saucepan and cover with boiling, salted water. Cover. Cook for about 20 minutes or until asparagus is tender. Drain and add the butter.

Steamed Fresh Asparagus (above)

ASPARAGUS AND SHRIMP ORIENTAL

2 tbsp. salad oil	1 lb. cooked deveined shrimp
1 med. onion, sliced	1 4-oz. can mushrooms
1 c. sliced celery	1 can water chestnuts
1/2 tsp. salt	2 tbsp. soy sauce
1/4 tsp. pepper	1 11-oz. can mandarin orange
2 tbsp. sugar	slices, drained
1 can asparagus, drained	

Heat the oil in a Chinese wok or electric skillet. Add the onion, celery, salt, pepper and sugar and cook, stirring until vegetables are crisp-tender. Add the asparagus, then shrimp. Drain and slice the mushrooms and water chestnuts and place over shrimp. Sprinkle with soy sauce and place orange slices on top. Cover and cook until mixture begins to steam. Reduce heat and simmer for about 12 minutes. Serve on rice. 6 servings.

Mrs. Eva G. Key, Mount Pleasant, South Carolina

SWEET AND SOUR ASPARAGUS

2/3 c. white vinegar	1 tsp. whole cloves
1/2 tsp. salt	1 tsp. celery seed
1/2 c. sugar	2 lge. cans green asparagus
3 sticks cinnamon	

Combine the vinegar, salt, sugar, spices and 1/2 cup water in a saucepan and bring to a boil. Pour over the asparagus. Cover and chill for 24 hours. Drain and serve. 6 servings.

Mrs. Mary J. Higgins, Marietta, Georgia

ASPARAGUS CASSEROLE WITH ALMONDS

1 14 1/2-oz. can green	Salt and pepper to taste
asparagus spears	1 can cream of mushroom soup
3 hard-cooked eggs, chopped	1 c. grated American cheese
6 slices crisp bacon, crumbled	1/2 c. bread crumbs (opt.)
1/2 c. slivered almonds	

Drain the asparagus and place in a shallow baking dish. Place eggs over asparagus. Add bacon and almonds and sprinkle with salt and pepper. Cover with soup and cheese and top with bread crumbs. Bake at 400 degrees for 30 minutes or until cheese is golden brown. 6-8 servings.

Mrs. Madge C. Kivett, Ramseur, North Carolina

CONGEALED ASPARAGUS SALAD WITH DRESSING

3/4 c. sugar	1/2 c. white vinegar
1 1/2 c. water	2 pkg. unflavored gelatin

1/2 tsp. salt
2 pimentos, chopped
1 sm. can asparagus tips,
    drained

Juice of 1/2 lemon
2 tsp. grated onion
1 c. chopped celery

Mix the sugar, 1 cup water and vinegar in a saucepan and bring to a boil. Soften the gelatin in remaining water. Add the gelatin and salt to vinegar mixture and stir until dissolved. Cool. Add remaining ingredients and pour into a mold. Chill until firm.

Dressing

1 c. sour cream
1/4 c. lemon juice
2 tbsp. sugar
1 tsp. salt
Cayenne pepper to taste

1/2 tsp. celery salt
1/2 tsp. paprika
1 tsp. dry mustard
1/4 tsp. garlic salt

Combine all ingredients in a bowl and blend with a rotary beater until smooth and thick. Serve with salad.

Jimmie Garvin Harris, Aiken, South Carolina

FRESH ASPARAGUS WITH CREAM SAUCE

2 lb. fresh asparagus
1/4 c. margarine or butter
1/4 c. flour
3/4 c. milk

3/4 c. cream
2 hard-boiled eggs, minced
2 tbsp. fresh lemon juice

Cook the asparagus in boiling, salted water until tender, then drain. Keep warm. Melt the margarine in a saucepan. Add the flour and mix well. Stir in the milk and cream and cook, stirring constantly, until smooth and thick. Reserve 1 teaspoon egg. Add remaining egg to sauce and mix well. Place the asparagus in a serving dish and sprinkle with lemon juice. Place the cream sauce in a serving bowl and sprinkle with reserved egg.

Fresh Asparagus with Cream Sauce (above)

SWEET AND SOUR CELERY

3 c. sliced celery	3/4 tsp. salt
1 egg, beaten	1/8 tsp. pepper
2 tbsp. flour	2 tbsp. vinegar
2 tbsp. sugar	1/4 c. sour cream

Cook the celery in boiling salted water until tender and drain. Blend the egg, flour, sugar, salt and pepper in a saucepan. Blend in the vinegar and 1 cup water. Cook over medium heat, stirring constantly, until the mixture comes to a boil. Remove from the heat and add the sour cream. Add to the celery and mix well. 6 servings.

Mrs. Tom Daniel, Van Buren, Arkansas

CELERY COLESLAW

1 unpeeled apple	2 tbsp. sugar
3 c. thinly sliced celery	1/2 tsp. salt
1/2 c. grated carrots	2 tbsp. vinegar
1/2 c. mayonnaise	

Core and chop the apple, then combine the celery, carrots and apple in a bowl. Mix the mayonnaise, sugar, salt and vinegar and fold into celery mixture. Chill for at least 30 minutes. 6 servings.

Mrs. Norman Steele, Fargo, Oklahoma

FRENCH BRAISED CELERY

2 c. cut-up celery	1 tsp. salt
4 sprigs of parsley	1/4 tsp. pepper
4 slices onion	2 strips bacon, chopped
1/2 c. bouillon	Buttered bread crumbs

Place the celery, parsley, onion slices and bouillon in a casserole and sprinkle with salt, pepper and bacon. Cover. Bake at 375 degrees for 30 minutes. Sprinkle with the buttered bread crumbs. Bake, uncovered, for 10 minutes longer or until the crumbs are browned. 4 servings.

Mary Ann Hribek, Giddings, Texas

STUFFED CELERY

1 tbsp. salad dressing	10 stuffed olives, finely chopped
1 sm. package cream cheese	1 med. bunch celery
1/4 c. sour cream	

Cream the salad dressing with the cream cheese and sour cream, then add the olives. Mix well and stuff into the celery. Arrange on lettuce-lined serving tray with additional olives. 8 servings.

Irene Clanton, Memphis, Tennessee

ORIENTAL CELERY SAUTE

1 4-oz. can sliced mushrooms
1 5-oz. can water chestnuts
2 tbsp. butter
2 c. diagonally sliced celery

1/2 c. sliced green onions
1 tsp. seasoned salt
1/4 tsp. seasoned pepper

Drain the mushrooms. Drain and slice the water chestnuts. Melt the butter in a saucepan. Add the mushrooms, water chestnuts, celery, green onions and seasonings. Saute for 2 minutes or until tender crisp, stirring constantly. 4 servings.

Jane Sproggin, Raleigh, North Carolina

CELERY AND CHEESE CASSEROLE

1 bunch fresh Florida celery
3 tbsp. butter or margarine
1/4 c. water
1/2 tsp. crumbled tarragon
   leaves

2 tbsp. flour
1/2 c. milk
1 can cream of chicken soup
1/2 c. grated Cheddar cheese
1/4 tsp. paprika

Preheat oven to 350 degrees. Trim the celery and cut ribs into 1/2-inch diagonal pieces. Combine the celery and 1 tablespoon butter, water and tarragon in a medium saucepan and bring to boiling point. Cover. Reduce heat and simmer for 10 minutes. Turn into a 2-quart casserole and set aside. Heat remaining butter in the same saucepan. Stir in the flour and brown lightly. Add the milk gradually and cook, stirring, until smooth. Add the undiluted soup and heat through. Stir in the cheese. Pour over the celery and mix lightly. Sprinkle with paprika. Bake for 15 minutes or until bubbly. Serve hot. 6-8 servings.

Celery and Cheese Casserole (above)

FAR EAST CELERY

4 c. celery slices
1 5-oz. can water chestnuts
1 can cream of chicken soup
1/4 c. diced pimento

1/2 c. soft bread crumbs
1/4 c. toasted slivered almonds
2 tbsp. melted butter

Cook the celery slices in a small amount of boiling water for about 8 minutes, until just tender and drain. Drain the chestnuts and slice thin. Mix the celery, water chestnuts, soup and pimento in a 1-quart casserole. Toss the bread crumbs with the almonds and melted butter and sprinkle over the celery mixture. Bake at 350 degrees for 35 minutes or until hot. 6 servings.

Mrs. Vivian Hammond, Greenville, South Carolina

CELERY AMANDINE

4 c. finely sliced celery
1/2 c. butter
1 tbsp. chopped chives
1 tbsp. grated onion
Salt and pepper to taste

1 1/2 tbsp. flour
1 c. light cream
1/2 c. chicken bouillon
1 c. sliced almonds

Simmer the celery, butter, chives, onion, salt and pepper in a covered saucepan over low heat until tender. Remove from heat. Combine the flour with a small amount of the cream and stir into the celery mixture. Add the remaining cream and bouillon. Cook over low heat, stirring constantly, until thickened. Boil for 1 minute. Add almonds and additional seasoning, if desired.

Mrs. Alice Todd, Little Rock, Arkansas

CELERY AND PECAN RING

1 c. fine dry bread crumbs
1 1/2 c. ground celery
2 tbsp. ground parsley
3/4 c. ground pecans
1/3 c. ground onion
1/3 c. ground green pepper

3 lge. eggs
3 tbsp. melted butter
1 tsp. salt
Pepper
1 1/2 c. milk

Combine all ingredients in a bowl and beat thoroughly. Pour into a well-buttered 8 1/2-inch ring mold. Let stand for 30 minutes. Place in a larger pan containing hot water. Bake in a 350-degree oven for 1 hour. Let stand in hot water for 10 minutes before unmolding. Serve at once with the center filled with creamed sweetbreads and mushrooms. 6-8 servings.

Mrs. Bert Derry, Orangeburg, South Carolina

BAKED CELERY

3 slices lean bacon, chopped
1 onion, thinly sliced

2 tbsp. chopped parsley
1 sm. garlic clove, crushed

8 med. stalks celery
1 c. beef consomme

1/4 c. fine bread crumbs
3 tbsp. melted butter

Place the bacon, onion, parsley and garlic in a well-greased shallow baking dish and arrange the celery stalks on top. Add the consomme and cover. Bake at 325 degrees for about 1 hour or until the celery is tender. Saute the bread crumbs in butter and sprinkle over the celery during last 10 minutes of baking. 4 servings.

Julia Stevens, Columbia, South Carolina

CELERY WITH ALMONDS

1 qt. chopped cooked celery
1 pt. medium cream sauce
1 can cream of chicken soup

1/2 c. grated Parmesan cheese
1 c. blanched slivered almonds

Drain the celery and combine with remaining ingredients. Pour into a buttered casserole. Bake at 400 degrees until golden brown. 6 servings.

Mrs. John Guthrie, Baltimore, Maryland

CELERY CROQUETTES

1 lge. eggplant, peeled
1 med. onion
3 c. diced celery
3/4 tsp. salt
1/8 tsp. white pepper

4 c. soft bread crumbs
2 eggs, slightly beaten
Dry bread crumbs
Oil

Dice the eggplant and onion. Combine the eggplant, onion, celery, salt and pepper. Place in a saucepan and add 1 inch boiling water. Cover and cook for 5 minutes. Drain. Add the soft bread crumbs and eggs and blend well. Drop by spoonfuls into dry bread crumbs. Roll and shape into balls. Fry in deep oil at 375 degrees until golden. Serve with lime wedges and chilled shrimp. May be frozen before frying. 6-8 servings.

Celery Croquettes (above)

FRESH CELERY PARMESAN

2 c. sliced celery	2 tbsp. butter
Chicken stock or water	1/8 tsp. ground white pepper
Salt to taste	1/3 c. grated Parmesan cheese

Place the celery in a saucepan with 1 inch of boiling stock and salt. Cover and bring to the boiling point. Cook for 10 minutes or until tender crisp. Drain well and place in a shallow pan. Dot with butter and sprinkle with pepper and cheese. Broil until flecked with brown. 6 servings.

Mrs. Mary Williams, Mobile, Alabama

CELERY AND CHESTNUTS

4 c. diced celery	Pimento
1 can water chestnuts	Bread crumbs
1 can cream of chicken soup	Butter
Dash of soy sauce	Slivered almonds

Simmer the celery for 5 to 10 minutes or until just tender and drain well. Drain and slice the chestnuts. Combine cooked celery with the soup and water chestnuts. Add soy sauce and enough pimento to add color. Place in a shallow buttered baking dish. Sprinkle with bread crumbs. Dot with butter and sprinkle with almonds. Bake at 350 degrees for 30 minutes.

Mrs. Richard C. Johnson, St. Petersburg, Florida

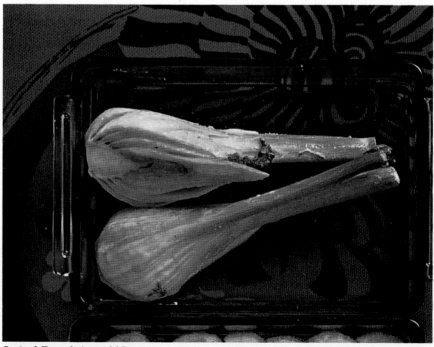

Braised Fennels (page 105)

CHARD WITH MUSHROOM SAUCE

2 lb. Chinese chard	1 1/2 tbsp. soy sauce
5 tbsp. salad oil	1 4-oz. can mushroom stems and
Salt to taste	pieces
1/2 tsp. brown sugar	1/3 c. bamboo shoots
2 c. soup stock	

Discard the outer leaves from the chard and wash thoroughly. Cut into 1 1/2 or 2-inch lengths. Saute the chard in hot oil in a skillet for 4 or 5 minutes, stirring constantly. Add the salt and brown sugar and cook for 1 minute longer. Add the soup stock, soy sauce, mushrooms and bamboo shoots. Cook for about 5 minutes longer, stirring constantly.

Mrs. Dorothy S. Moon, Newport News, Virginia

CHINESE CHARD

2 1/2 lb. Chinese chard	1/2 tsp. sugar
6 tbsp. chicken fat	1/2 c. chicken consomme
1/2 tsp. salt	

Discard the outer leaves from the chard, then wash the chard thoroughly. Dry and cut into 2-inch lengths. Melt the chicken fat in a skillet over high heat. Add the chard and cook, stirring constantly for 6 to 8 minutes. Add the salt, sugar and consomme and cook, stirring, for 2 minutes longer.

Mrs. Claire Boyd, Boonsboro, Maryland

SAUTEED FENNEL

1 1/2 lb. fennel	1 clove of garlic
1 tsp. salt	2 tbsp. olive oil
6 c. water	Pepper to taste

Select fennel with white hearts and dark green leaves. Wash thoroughly and remove tough outer leaves. Cut the tender leaves in half, and cut the hearts in quarters. Bring the salt and water to a boil and add the fennel. Cover and cook over low heat for about 10 minutes or until tender. Saute the garlic in hot oil until brown, then remove the garlic and add the fennel. Saute for 3 minutes and dust with pepper. Serve immediately.

Mrs. H. M. Green, Raleigh, North Carolina

BRAISED FENNELS

3 fennels	Dash of pepper
2 tbsp. butter or margarine	1/2 c. water
Salt to taste	

Rinse the fennels and cut lengthwise. Brown the butter in a saucepan. Place the fennels in the saucepan and season with salt and pepper. Cook over low heat until the fennels are golden brown. Add the water and simmer for about 20 minutes. 4 servings.

vegetable fruits

What are vegetable fruits? In a botanical sense, they *are* fruits — they develop from a flower — but they have been served as luscious vegetables to generations of appreciative families. Included among them are bell or green peppers, corn, cucumbers, eggplant, as well as okra, squash, and tomatoes. Southern homemakers have turned their considerable culinary talents toward developing unforgettable vegetable dishes with these foods . . . dishes which have won the approval of families and friends and are now featured in the following section.

Peppers can play an important role at your next party when you serve Sweet Pepper Fondue, a blend of flavors and textures certain to put everyone in a happy mood. Sparkle up your family's mealtime with brilliant purple eggplant. Its flavor blends well with many different foods, as in Eggplant and Shrimp Casserole, a special favorite in southern coastal towns. Another popular vegetable fruit is okra. First brought to the Southland by Africans, okra thrives in the hot and humid climate of this region. Serve Fried Okra or Okra Pilau — and learn why thousands of southern women depend on this flavorful vegetable to highlight their meals.

These are just some of the delightful recipes waiting for you in the pages of this section. Home-tested and family-approved, these favorites will add a fillip of southern flavor to your table!

STUFFED GREEN PEPPER

6 lge. green peppers	1/4 tsp. pepper
3 c. cooked ground beef	2 c. soft bread crumbs
1 med. onion, minced	1/4 c. melted butter

Cut a thin slice from the stem end of the peppers and remove the seeds. Cook the peppers in boiling salted water for about 8 minutes or until tender. Drain and place in a baking dish. Mix the ground beef, onion, pepper, bread crumbs and butter in a large mixing bowl. Fill the peppers with the ground beef mixture. Do not pack tightly. Pour 1/2 cup water in bottom of the baking dish. Bake for 30 minutes in a 350-degree oven.

Mrs. Johnie Anderson, Quinton, Oklahoma

BELL PEPPERS ETOFFE

3 bell peppers	1 boiled egg, chopped
2/3 c. rice	2 tbsp. grated onion
1 lge. can deviled ham	Salt and pepper to taste

Remove the tops and seeds from the bell peppers. Parboil until tender. Cook the rice according to package directions and combine with the deviled ham, egg, onion, salt and pepper. Stuff peppers with the deviled ham mixture and place in a pan with about 1 inch of hot water. Tops of peppers may be chopped into stuffing or placed on top. Bake in 400-degree oven for about 30 minutes or until stuffing seems puffy.

Mrs. Emmett Turner, Jefferson, Texas

AMERICAN-STYLE GREEN PEPPERS

1 c. cut-up snap beans	1/4 c. flour
1 c. sliced fresh carrots	1 1/2 c. milk
1 c. sliced celery	1 c. grated Cheddar cheese
5 lge. green bell peppers	1/2 tsp. salt
1/4 c. butter or margarine	1/8 tsp. pepper

Cook the beans, carrots and celery together in a small amount of boiling salted water for about 10 minutes or just until tender, then drain. Wash the bell peppers. Cut the tops off and scoop out the seeds. Parboil for 10 minutes in 1-inch boiling salted water. Remove from water and drain well. Melt the butter and blend in the flour. Add the milk gradually and cook, stirring, until thickened. Stir in the cheese, salt, pepper and vegetables. Fill the green pepper shells with the creamed vegetables. Place in a greased shallow baking dish. Bake, uncovered, in 350-degree oven for 50 minutes. 5 servings.

Mrs. L. R. Bonner, Odessa, Texas

SWEET PEPPER FONDUE

1 clove of garlic, split
2 c. riesling or Rhine wine
1 lb. Swiss cheese, shredded
2 tbsp. flour

1/2 tsp. salt
1/4 tsp. pepper
Green and red pepper squares

Rub a fondue pot with garlic. Pour in the riesling and heat until riesling begins to bubble. Mix the cheese with flour and add to riesling gradually. Cook, stirring, until cheese has melted. Add the salt and pepper and heat through. Place the fondue pot over a flame. Spear the pepper squares with bamboo skewers and dip into fondue.

Mrs. Ed Luther, Newark, Delaware

STUFFED BELL PEPPERS

6 fresh green peppers
6 ears of fresh corn
1 lb. ground beef

1/4 c. chopped fresh onion
Salt and pepper to taste

Cut tops from the green peppers and remove seeds and membranes. Cook in boiling, salted water until partially done, then drain. Cut the corn from cobs and place in a skillet. Add 1/2 cup water and cook over low heat, stirring frequently, until water has evaporated. Add the ground beef, onion, salt and pepper and cook until beef is brown, stirring occasionally. Stuff the green peppers with corn mixture and place in a baking pan. Bake at 350 degrees for about 30 minutes. Green peppers may be stuffed with other mixtures, if desired.

Stuffed Bell Peppers (above)

GREEN PEPPER CASSEROLE

1 1/2 c. milk	2 tbsp. butter
1 c. cooked chopped green peppers	1 c. shredded Cheddar cheese
1 c. cracker crumbs	Salt and pepper to taste

Combine all the ingredients in a greased casserole. Bake at 350 degrees for about 30 minutes. 6-8 servings.

Doris C. Mountjoy, Stanford, Kentucky

CORN-STUFFED SWEET PEPPERS

6 med. green peppers	1/4 tsp. pepper
1 1/4 tsp. salt	1/8 tsp. garlic powder
3 c. corn, cut from cob	1 tsp. chili powder
1 c. diced tomatoes	3 tbsp. flour
1 1/2 tsp. instant minced onion	2 tbsp. melted butter or margarine

Slice tops from the green peppers and remove seeds and membranes carefully. Place in a saucepan and cover with boiling water. Add 1/2 teaspoon salt. Cover the saucepan and cook for 5 minutes. Drain. Combine remaining salt and remaining ingredients and spoon into the green peppers. Place in a baking pan. Bake at 375 degrees for 35 minutes or until done.

Mrs. H. E. Washington, Las Cruces, New Mexico

BOSTON-STYLE BAKED CORN

1 tsp. dry mustard	1 sm. onion, diced
1/2 tsp. salt	2 12-oz. cans whole kernel corn, drained
2 tbsp. brown sugar	2 to 3 slices bacon, diced
1 c. catsup	

Combine the mustard, salt, sugar and catsup in a medium bowl and add the onion and corn. Mix thoroughly. Pour the mixture into a greased 1 1/2-quart casserole. Top with the bacon pieces. Bake in 350-degree oven for 40 minutes or until the bacon is done and the corn is heated. 6-8 servings.

Cathie Miller, Jackson, Mississippi

COUNTRY CLUB CORN

1/4 c. milk	1 stick margarine
1 can cream-style corn	8 to 10 soda crackers
Salt and pepper to taste	

Mix the milk and corn and add salt and pepper. Pour in buttered casserole. Cut the margarine in small pieces and arrange on top of corn. Break the crackers in small pieces and place on top of casserole. Bake at 350 degrees until slightly brown on top. 6-8 servings.

Charlotte McCracken, Sentinel, Oklahoma

CORN CASSEROLE

8 sm. ears of corn
2 eggs, beaten
1 tbsp. grated onion
1 tbsp. butter

3/4 tsp. salt
Dash of pepper
3/4 c. milk

Scrape the kernels from the corn. Add the eggs and stir in grated onion. Add the butter, salt, pepper and milk. Pour into a buttered baking dish. Bake at 300 degrees for 40 minutes.

Mrs. A. M. Byrd, Panama City, Florida

FRESH SOUTHERN CORN PUDDING

2 c. fresh corn, cut from cob
2 tsp. sugar
1 1/2 tsp. salt
1/8 tsp. pepper

3 eggs, lightly beaten
2 tbsp. butter or margarine
2 c. milk

Preheat oven to 350 degrees. Combine the corn, sugar, salt and pepper in a bowl. Add the eggs and mix well. Add the butter to milk in a saucepan and heat until butter is melted. Blend with corn mixture. Turn into a greased 1-quart casserole and place in a pan of hot water. Bake for 1 hour or until a knife inserted in center comes out clean. Garnish with fresh parsley. 6 servings.

Fresh Southern Corn Pudding (above)

CORN SOUFFLE

2 c. cooked fresh corn	2 c. rich milk
1 tsp. salt	3 or 4 eggs, well beaten
1 tsp. sugar	4 tbsp. butter, melted
1 tbsp. cornstarch	1 green pepper, cut in rings

Combine the corn, salt and sugar. Dissolve the cornstarch in a small amount of milk, then add with remaining milk to the corn mixture. Add the eggs and butter. Pour into a buttered casserole and top with pepper rings. Bake at 375 degrees for 45 minutes or until set. 4-6 servings.

Mrs. Curtis E. Connor, Daingerfield, Texas

CORN PIE

1 1/4 c. fine cracker crumbs	1 c. milk
Butter or margarine, melted	1 can whole kernel corn
1/4 c. chopped green pepper	1/2 tsp. salt
1 tbsp. finely chopped onion	1 tsp. sugar
2 tbsp. flour	2 eggs, slightly beaten

Blend 1 cup cracker crumbs and 1/2 cup melted butter and press evenly on bottom and sides of baking dish. Cook pepper and onion in 2 tablespoons butter until onion is transparent. Blend in the flour and cook until bubbly. Add the milk and cook, stirring constantly, until thickened. Add the corn, salt, sugar and eggs. Mix well and pour into the crust. Top with remaining crumbs. Bake at 400 degrees for about 25 minutes or until firm. 6 servings.

Mrs. Robert E. McNair, Columbia, South Carolina

CORN SPOON

3 eggs, separated	2 tbsp. butter or margarine
3/4 c. cornmeal	2 c. cream-style corn
3/4 tsp. salt	3/4 tsp. baking powder
1 1/4 c. milk, scalded	

Grease a 2-quart baking dish. Beat the egg whites at room temperature till stiff but not dry and beat the yolks till thick and lemon colored. Stir the cornmeal and salt into the scalded milk, beating hard. Stir till consistency of thick mush. Blend in the butter and corn and add baking powder. Fold in the yolks, then whites. Pour into a baking dish. Bake at 375 degrees for 35 minutes or till puffy and golden brown and knife inserted in center comes out clean. 5-6 servings.

Mrs. Sharon Kay Patterson, Little Rock, Arkansas

DANISH CUCUMBERS

1 lge. cucumber	2 tbsp. sugar
1 tsp. salt	1/3 c. vinegar

Wash and slice the cucumbers thin. Sprinkle with the salt and sugar and add the vinegar. Press the slices with the back of a spoon until salad is quite juicy.

Mrs. M. N. Stringer, Bay Springs, Mississippi

CUCUMBER DELIGHT

2 c. apple cider vinegar
2 c. water
1 c. sugar
3 tbsp. salt

Cucumbers
1 sm. onion, sliced
1 garlic clove, chopped

Combine the vinegar, water, sugar and salt and bring to a boil. Set aside to cool. Wash, peel and slice the cucumbers. Place the onion and garlic in the bottom of a jar. Add the cucumbers to jar, filling to top. Fill the jar with vinegar mixture and seal. Keep in refrigerator for 3 days before serving. Leftover vinegar may be used again.

Mrs. Elizabeth Evans, Disputanta, Virginia

FRIED EGGPLANT

2 sm. eggplant
1 egg, beaten
1 c. bread crumbs

1 tsp. salt
Dash of pepper

Rinse the eggplant and slice. Dip in egg. Mix the bread crumbs, salt and pepper and coat eggplant slices with bread crumbs. Fry in small amount of fat in a skillet over low heat for about 3 minutes on each side. 4 servings.

Fried Eggplant (above)

EGGPLANT CASSEROLE DELUXE

2 med. eggplant
1 lge. onion, chopped
2 garlic buds, chopped
2 tsp. salt
2 tsp. pepper
1 tsp. fine herbs

1 pt. oysters
4 tbsp. butter
2 lb. ground round
1/4 c. Parmesan cheese
6 eggs, well beaten

Peel the eggplant and cut in cubes. Simmer the cubed eggplant, onion, garlic, salt, pepper and herbs in a small amount of water and do not overcook. Saute the oysters in a small amount of butter until the edges curl. Add the butter, ground round, cheese, eggs and oysters to the eggplant mixture and pour in a casserole. Bake in a pan of water at 350 degrees for 1 hour and 30 minutes to 2 hours or until set.

Mrs. L. R. Baker, Harlingen, Texas

EGGPLANT AND SHRIMP CASSEROLE

2 med. eggplant, cooked
1 lb. shelled deveined shrimp
1 c. wet crumbled French bread
2 slices crisp bacon
1/2 c. chopped green pepper
1/2 c. chopped parsley

1/4 c. chopped celery
1 lge. onion, chopped fine
2 garlic cloves, chopped fine
Salt and pepper to taste
Bread crumbs
Margarine

Peel the eggplant and mash in a large mixing bowl. Cut the shrimp in small pieces and add to eggplant. Squeeze bread dry. Break bacon in pieces. Add bread, bacon and remaining ingredients except crumbs and margarine to eggplant mixture and mix well. Stir in 1/4 cup melted margarine and place in a casserole. Cover with bread crumbs and dot with 2 tablespoons margarine. Bake at 350 degrees for about 1 hour. 6 servings.

Mrs. Rose Singer, New Orleans, Louisiana

GRECIAN MOUSSAKA CASSEROLE

1 med. eggplant
1/2 c. oil
4 med. onions, sliced
3 cloves of garlic, minced
2 tbsp. butter
1 lb. ground beef
1/2 tsp. salt

1/2 tsp. thyme
1/2 tsp. oregano
1/2 c. white wine
1/2 c. tomatoes
2 egg whites
1/2 c. fine bread crumbs
Bechamel Sauce

Slice the unpeeled eggplant in 1/2-inch slices and fry in oil until brown on both sides. Cook the onions and garlic in the butter until tender, then add the ground beef, salt, herbs, wine and tomatoes. Cool and add the unbeaten egg whites and

1/4 cup bread crumbs. Grease a 2-quart casserole and sprinkle sides and bottom with remaining crumbs. Fill with alternate layers of eggplant and ground beef mixture. Top with Bechamel Sauce. Bake in 350-degree oven for 1 hour.

Bechamel Sauce

2 tbsp. butter	1 1/2 c. milk
2 tbsp. flour	2 egg yolks
1/2 tsp. salt	1/8 tsp. nutmeg

Melt the butter in the top of a double boiler, then add flour and salt. Add the milk, stirring constantly, to make thick cream sauce. Mix a small amount of the sauce with well-beaten egg yolks and return to the pan. Add the nutmeg.

Mrs. V. I. Gray, Miami, Florida

RATATOUILLE

1/3 c. olive oil	1 lge. green pepper, cut in
1 garlic clove, mashed	strips
2 med. onions, thinly sliced	1 tsp. monosodium glutamate
3 sm. zucchini, sliced	1 tsp. salt
1 med. eggplant, cubed	1/4 tsp. pepper
3 ripe tomatoes, coarsely	1/2 tsp. dried leaf oregano
chopped	

Heat the olive oil in a large skillet. Add the garlic and onions and cook until onions are tender but not brown. Layer remaining vegetables in the skillet, sprinkling each layer with monosodium glutamate, salt, pepper and oregano, then cover. Cook over low heat for 20 to 25 minutes or until vegetables are tender. Serve immediately or chill and serve cold. 6 servings.

Ratatouille (above)

EASY FRIED EGGPLANT

1 med. eggplant	**1/4 tsp. pepper**
1 c. meal	**Shortening**
1/2 tsp. salt	

Peel and slice the eggplant in 1/4-inch slices crosswise. Mix the meal, salt and pepper and dip the eggplant slices in the seasoned meal. Place in 1 layer of 1/4 inch of 350-degree shortening. Let brown, then turn and brown the other side. Remove from shortening immediately.

Mrs. Dendby Curry, Minerva, Texas

KING OF NAPLES

1 eggplant	**6 oz. spaghetti, cooked**
2/3 c. cream	**1 c. shredded cheese**
1 lge. can tomatoes	**Salt and pepper to taste**

Peel and slice the eggplant. Pour cream into a buttered baking dish. Add the eggplant slices, tomatoes, spaghetti and cheese in layers, ending with cheese. Season each layer with salt and pepper. Bake at 325 degrees for 1 hour and 30 minutes. 8-10 servings.

Betty Smith, Beaumont, Texas

EGGPLANT SOUFFLE

1 1 to 1 1/4-lb. eggplant	**1/8 tsp. pepper**
2 c. cold water	**1 c. cracker crumbs**
1/2 c. nonfat dry milk solids	**1/3 lb. grated sharp Cheddar**
2 eggs, well beaten	**cheese**
1 tsp. salt	**2 tbsp. butter or margarine**

Peel and cut eggplant into 1/2-inch cubes. Cook in water over medium heat for about 15 minutes or till tender. Drain and reserve 1 1/2 cups liquid. Add dry milk, eggs, salt, pepper, cracker crumbs, reserved liquid, cheese and butter and pour into a 1 1/2 or 2-quart casserole. Bake in 350-degree oven for about 30 minutes or until knife inserted in middle comes out clean. Serve at once. 8 servings.

Sue Jones, Flora, Mississippi

EGGPLANT AND LAMB CASSEROLE

1 peeled eggplant, sliced	**1/2 tsp. chervil**
1 1/2 lb. ground lamb	**1/2 tsp. marjoram**
1 med. onion, chopped	**1 1/2 c. consomme**
3 tbsp. oil	**2 c. canned tomatoes**
Salt and pepper to taste	**1 1/2 c. rice**

Soak the eggplant in salted water for 15 minutes and drain. Cook the lamb and onion in oil in a skillet until brown, then stir in the salt, pepper, chervil, marjoram, consomme and tomatoes. Brown the rice in a skillet. Place alternate layers of eggplant, lamb mixture and rice in a casserole and cover. Bake at 350 degrees for 1 hour and 30 minutes. 6 servings.

Mrs. C. E. Crabill, Cleburne, Texas

EGGPLANT WITH SOUR CREAM

Eggplant	1 clove of garlic
French dressing	Sour cream with minced chives

Cut the eggplant into 3/4-inch slices. Marinate in the French dressing with garlic for 1 hour, then drain. Bake at 450 degrees for 20 minutes. Remove from oven and spread with the sour cream. Return to oven with door open and heat for 5 minutes. Serve warm.

Mrs. Dorothy A. Foster, Mathews, Virginia

EGGPLANT CASSEROLE

1 lge. eggplant	1/4 tsp. allspice
Salt to taste	Pepper to taste
1/2 c. toasted ground pecans	4 tbsp. margarine
1/2 c. bread crumbs	1 c. milk
1 tbsp. flour	

Peel the eggplant and cut in 1/2-inch slices. Sprinkle with salt and let set for 1 hour. Rinse with cold water and drain. Mix the pecans, bread crumbs, flour and allspice. Sprinkle eggplant slices with salt and pepper and dip in pecan mixture. Arrange in a baking dish and dot with margarine. Bake at 350 degrees for about 20 minutes until light brown. Add the milk and bake for 30 minutes longer or until milk is absorbed. Serve hot. 6-8 servings.

Mrs. J. R. Porter, Moselle, Mississippi

EGGPLANT PATTIES

1 med. eggplant	1 1/2 tsp. salt
2 med. potatoes	1 tsp. sage
2 c. chopped celery	2 beaten eggs
1/4 c. chopped onion	Whole wheat cereal flakes
3 tbsp. soy sauce	

Wash, peel and dice the eggplant and potatoes. Place eggplant, potatoes, celery and onion in a saucepan and add 2 cups water. Cook over low heat until water is absorbed and vegetables are tender. Pour the mixture into a mixing bowl and add soy sauce, salt, sage and eggs. Add enough whole wheat flakes to form patties. Cook on oiled griddle at 350 degrees until brown. Serve with plain or mushroom gravy.

Mrs. E. L. Oden, Cleburne, Texas

Okra with Grapefruit-Butter Sauce (below)

OKRA WITH GRAPEFRUIT-BUTTER SAUCE

**1/2   6-oz. can frozen Florida
    grapefruit juice concentrate**
4 tbsp. butter or margarine
1/4 tsp. hot sauce

1 tsp. instant minced onion
**1   10-oz. package frozen
    whole okra**

Thaw the grapefruit juice. Melt the butter with hot sauce and onion in a saucepan over low heat. Stir in the undiluted grapefruit juice concentrate and heat through. Cook the okra according to package directions and place in a bowl. Pour the grapefruit sauce over okra. Garnish with grapefruit sections, if desired.

FRIED OKRA

6 to 8 sm. pods of okra
1/2 to 1 c. cornmeal

1/4 c. bacon fat

Wash the okra, then cut off the ends and slice to desired thickness. Toss the okra with meal until coated. Fry in the fat over medium heat for 25 minutes or until brown and crisp. 4 servings.

Mrs. Ruth Ragsdale, Richmond, Virginia

CORRIE'S OLD-TIME OKRA

1 lb. fresh okra
1 green pepper
1 1/2 tsp. salt

3 lge. fresh tomatoes
1 tsp. sugar
5 to 6 strips bacon

Place the okra in a cheesecloth bag. Soak in boiling water for 1 minute, then plunge immediately into cold water. Drain thoroughly and slice. Spread in 10 x 6 x 2-inch casserole. Cut the pepper in rings and place on the okra. Sprinkle with half the salt. Peel and slice the tomatoes and lay on top of the pepper. Sprinkle with remaining salt and sugar. Top with the bacon. Bake at 400 degrees for 1 hour and 30 minutes. 4-6 servings.

Pansy Maddox, Vidalia, Georgia

BOILED OKRA

1 qt. tender okra with 1/2-in. stems	1 tbsp. bacon drippings
1 tbsp. cider vinegar	Salt

Place the okra in a pan with cold water to just cover. Bring to a boil and add the vinegar. Do not stir okra while cooking. Boil until fork tender. Add the drippings and salt to taste. Lift okra from pan carefully to serve.

Mrs. Pearl Burbank, El Dorado, Arkansas

BAKED GINGER PUMPKIN

1 2-lb. pumpkin	1/4 c. chopped preserved ginger
1/2 c. butter	Salt to taste
1/4 c. brown sugar	Melted butter

Cut the pumpkin into serving-sized wedges. Peel and discard the seeds and fibers. Melt the butter and stir in the sugar and ginger. Score the wedges with a knife and spread them with the butter mixture. Sprinkle with salt. Place the pumpkin in 1/2 inch water in a shallow baking pan. Bake at 350 degrees for 1 hour and 30 minutes, basting frequently with melted butter.

Mrs. Chris Payne, Clanton, Alabama

ICED GREEN PUMPKIN PICKLE

7 lb. pumpkin rind	1 tsp. powdered cloves
3 c. lime	4 tbsp. whole cloves
5 lb. sugar	Green food coloring
3 pt. cider vinegar	

Dice and peel the pumpkin rind. Dissolve the lime in 2 gallons water. Soak the pumpkin in the lime solution for 24 hours, stirring occasionally to keep lime in suspension. Drain and soak in clear water for 4 hours, changing water each hour. Combine the sugar, vinegar, cloves and enough food coloring to obtain desired tint. Bring to a boil and pour over the pumpkin. Let stand overnight. Bring to a boil again, then pack in jars and seal.

Mrs. Wimbric Batton, Charleston, South Carolina

STEAMED PUMPKIN WITH CORN

1 sm. pumpkin	2 tbsp. chopped onion
Salt and pepper to taste	16 oz. cream cheese
Monosodium glutamate	1 can whole kernel corn
Butter	2 tbsp. Worcestershire sauce
6 slices bacon	

Steam the pumpkin until tender, then drain and mash. Add salt, pepper, mono-sodium glutamate and butter as for mashed potatoes. Fry the bacon until crisp and chop fine. Fry the onion in the bacon drippings. Add the cream cheese and stir until melted. Add the pumpkin, bacon, corn and Worcestershire sauce and mix well. Pat mixture into a baking dish. Cover and keep hot until ready to serve. 8 servings.

Mrs. M. Jean Henk, Biloxi, Mississippi

FLUFFY GINGER PUMPKIN

1 ripe pumpkin	Sugar
Butter	Pinch of ginger
Salt and pepper to taste	

Wash the pumpkin and cut into quarters, discarding the seeds and fibers. Place the pumpkin on a baking pan and fill to 1/2 inch with hot water. Bake at 350 degrees for about 1 hour and 30 minutes. Scrape the pulp from the rind and puree in a blender. Stir the puree over medium heat until almost dry. Season with butter, salt, pepper, sugar and ginger as desired. Puree may be used for pie filling.

Mrs. Martha Tanner, White Sulphur Springs, West Virginia

DILLED PUMPKIN

2 lb. pumpkin	1/2 tsp. salt
1 onion, finely chopped	1 tbsp. finely chopped dill
2 tbsp. melted butter	2 tsp. lemon juice
1 tbsp. flour	1/2 c. cream

Peel the pumpkin and cut in thin strips about 2 inches long. Brown the onion in the butter in a saucepan. Blend in the flour and stir in 1 cup hot water. Add the salt and dill and cook, stirring, until the sauce is smooth and thick. Add the pumpkin and cover. Cook over low heat for about 1 hour. Add the lemon juice and cream and cook until heated.

Mrs. J. B. Bethea, Columbia, South Carolina

ZUCCHINI FONDUE

1 c. soft butter or margarine	3 sm. garlic cloves, slivered
1/3 c. olive or peanut oil	5 c. sliced zucchini
1 2-oz. can anchovy fillets, well drained	Italian bread, sliced thin

Combine first 4 ingredients in blender container and blend until anchovies and garlic pieces are finely chopped. Pour into a metal fondue pot and place over medium heat until bubbly. Place fondue pot over low flame. Spear zucchini slices with fondue forks or long, heavy bamboo skewers and swirl in butter mixture until hot and lightly browned. Place slice of bread under zucchini as removed from butter mixture to catch drippings.

Wanda Moore, Bay Saint Louis, Mississippi

GARLIC ZUCCHINI

4 med. zucchini	Pinch of pepper
1/4 c. margarine, melted	Pinch of sugar
1/2 tsp. garlic salt	

Shred the zucchini coarsely. Combine with remaining ingredients and place in a skillet. Cover and cook over medium heat for 8 to 10 minutes, stirring occasionally. 4 servings.

Mrs. Earl Grant, Muskogee, Oklahoma

STUFFED ZUCCHINI

3 fresh zucchini	2 c. fresh corn, cut from cob
3 slices bacon	Salt and pepper to taste

Cut the zucchini in half and remove pulp. Cook in boiling, salted water until almost done, then drain. Fry the bacon in a skillet until crisp. Remove from skillet, then drain and crumble. Add the corn, salt, pepper and 1 cup water to drippings in skillet and cook over low heat, stirring frequently, until water has evaporated. Stir in the bacon, then place in cavities of zucchini. Place in a baking pan and pour small amount of water into the pan. Bake at 350 degrees for 30 minutes.

Stuffed Zucchini (above)

SQUASH CASSEROLE

3 sm. sausage patties	2 eggs, beaten slightly
2 med. onions	1 c. tomatoes
1 lb. squash	Cheese
Salt and pepper to taste	

Brown the sausage patties and place on paper towels to drain and cool. Slice the onions and squash. Boil together in a small amount of water until done. Drain and mash, then add salt and pepper. Break up the sausage patties and mix with the eggs, tomatoes, onions and squash. Pour into a casserole and top with cheese. Bake at 350 degrees for about 45 minutes.

Mrs. Joe Newsome, Fremont, North Carolina

CREAMY SQUASH CASSEROLE

2 lb. yellow squash, sliced	1 1/2 c. grated American
1/2 c. chopped onion	cheese
3/4 c. saltine cracker	Salt and pepper to taste
crumbs	3 eggs
2 tbsp. butter	1/2 c. evaporated milk

Cook the squash and onion in boiling water until tender, then drain. Add cracker crumbs, butter, 1 cup cheese, salt and pepper. Beat eggs lightly and add milk. Mix with squash mixture. Pour into a buttered casserole and sprinkle remaining cheese on top. Bake at 425 degrees until done. 8 servings.

Mrs. Wilma Dykes, Brandon, Florida

SQUASH-CARROT CASSEROLE

3 lb. yellow squash, sliced	1 carton sour cream
2 onions, chopped	1 sm. jar pimento strips
2 carrots, sliced	1/2 c. melted butter
Salt to taste	1 pkg. stuffing mix
2 cans cream of chicken soup	

Cook the squash, onions and carrots in boiling water until tender, then drain. Add remaining ingredients except butter and stuffing mix and mix well. Mix butter with stuffing mix and place half the mixture in a greased casserole. Add squash mixture and place remaining stuffing mixture on top. Bake at 375 degrees for 45 minutes. 12 servings.

Mrs. Weyman E. O'Neal, Conyers, Georgia

BUTTERNUT SQUASH CASSEROLE

3 med. butternut squash	1 c. cracker crumbs
1/4 c. minced onion	1/2 c. grated cheese

Salt and pepper to taste   1/4 c. cream or milk
1/4 c. butter   Paprika to taste

Slice the squash. Place alternate layers of squash, onion, cracker crumbs, cheese, salt, pepper and butter in a greased casserole. Add the cream and sprinkle with paprika. Cover. Bake at 375 degrees for 20 minutes. Uncover and bake for 10 minutes longer. 4-6 servings.

Mrs. Dorothy A. Foster, Mathews, Virginia

DANISH TOMATOES

Fresh tomatoes   Buttered croutons
Sugar to taste   Crumbled bleu cheese
Salt to taste

Cut the tops off tomatoes and cut almost through in wedges. Spread to resemble flowers. Sprinkle with sugar and salt and place in a shallow pan. Bake at 375 degrees for 10 minutes. Add the croutons and cheese. Bake until the cheese bubbles.

Rosemary Martine, Chattahoochee, Florida

BROILED FRESH TOMATOES

4 fresh tomatoes   Salt and pepper to taste
2 tbsp. melted butter   1/4 c. grated Parmesan cheese

Cut the tomatoes in thick slices and place in a greased shallow baking dish. Brush with butter and sprinkle with salt and pepper. Sprinkle with cheese. Broil about 6 inches from heat for about 15 minutes or until cheese is lightly browned.

Broiled Fresh Tomatoes (above)

Stuffed Fresh Tomatoes (below)

STUFFED FRESH TOMATOES

6 fresh tomatoes	1/4 c. half and half
2 c. cottage cheese	Salt to taste
1/4 c. chopped fresh chives	Mayonnaise
1/4 c. chopped fresh green onions	Fresh parsley

Cut each tomato 3/4 of the way down into 6 wedges, then separate wedges slightly. Mix the cottage cheese, chives, green onions, half and half and salt and place in center of each tomato. Garnish with mayonnaise and fresh parsley sprigs, if desired.

FRESH TOMATO CASSEROLE

6 med. fresh tomatoes	Salt to taste
1/2 c. chopped fresh celery	2 c. fresh corn, cut from cob
1/2 c. chopped fresh green pepper	3 hard-boiled eggs, sliced
1/2 c. chopped fresh onion	2 c. medium white sauce

Peel and chop 5 tomatoes. Place in a saucepan and add the celery, green pepper and onion. Cook, stirring occasionally, for 15 minutes, then stir in the salt. Place half the mixture in a casserole. Add half the corn. Add the eggs, then add half the white sauce. Add remaining tomato mixture and remaining corn. Cover with remaining white sauce. Bake at 350 degrees for about 45 minutes. Slice remaining tomato and place on casserole.

Photograph for this recipe on page 106.

TOMATO RICE

4 strips bacon
1/2 c. thinly sliced onion
2 1/2 c. peeled cubed tomatoes
1/4 green pepper, cut into strips
2 tsp. salt

1 tsp. paprika
1 clove of garlic, minced
Dash of pepper
2 1/2 c. cooked rice

Fry the bacon until crisp and remove from the pan. Add the onion, tomatoes, green pepper, salt, paprika, garlic and pepper to drippings and cook until the vegetables are transparent. Fold in the rice and crumbled bacon and place in a casserole. Bake at 350 degrees for 10 minutes or until heated through. Serve hot. 4-5 servings.

Ollie Lee Arter, Kiowa, Oklahoma

DELICIOUS CRAB-STUFFED TOMATOES

1 8-oz. package cream cheese
Mayonnaise
1 c. white crab meat
2 tsp. grated fresh onion

Dash of Worcestershire sauce
Salt to taste
2 lge. fresh tomatoes

Soften the cream cheese, then beat until smooth and fluffy. Add enough mayonnaise to moisten and mix well. Add the crab meat, onion, Worcestershire sauce and salt and mix well. Remove stem ends from the tomatoes and cut each tomato into 4 slices. Reserve 1 slice. Spread the crab mixture on remaining slices of tomato, then stack the slices, crab mixture side up. Place reserved tomato slice on top. Place on side on fresh greens in a serving dish and garnish with fresh cherry tomatoes.

Delicious Crab-Stuffed Tomatoes (above)

specialty vegetables

Unusual vegetables for special occasions — that's what is waiting for you in the pages which follow. Explore the epicurean world of seldom-served mushrooms . . . truffles . . . artichokes . . . and rare but delicious greens like fiddleheads, cardoons, and celeriac.

Southern homemakers are at home in natural gardens where many specialty vegetables grow — around marshes or in the woods which dot the Southland. Through generations of exciting experimentation, they have developed recipes which make the most of such gourmet delights.

Browse through this section and discover a highly-flavored recipe for Artichoke Hearts and Pecans — a dish you'll want to serve at your very next special luncheon or buffet. Transform Brussels sprouts with the addition of grapes — the recipe is waiting for you here.

And when you want to draw wondering comments from family and guests, prepare Sauteed Truffles. This much-admired delicacy takes on special flavors when lovingly sauteed. For great taste, of course you'll want to serve mushrooms — try Mushrooms with Bacon, a blend of flavors and textures certain to win compliments for you.

What an exciting chapter this is — one you'll depend on every time you want to mark an occasion as special . . . by serving specialty vegetables.

127

BUTTERED CELERIAC

1 1/4 lb. celeriac	Salt and pepper to taste
Butter	

Wash the celeriac thoroughly. Scrub with a brush to remove all traces of dirt and cut off root fibers. Cook, covered, in boiling salted water for 40 minutes to 1 hour. Drain and plunge into cold water. Peel and slice or dice as desired. Season with butter, salt and pepper and reheat to serve.

Mrs. F. J. Russell, Birmingham, Alabama

SUPERB CELERIAC SALAD

2 med. firm celeriacs	5 tbsp. mayonnaise or salad
2 tbsp. lemon juice	dressing
4 hard-cooked eggs	Salt to taste
1/4 c. chopped onion	Pimento-stuffed olives
1 tbsp. minced parsley	Paprika
1/8 tsp. pepper	

Peel the celeriac, cutting away root fibers and any adhering top growth. Cut in halves and cover with boiling salted water. Add 1 teaspoon lemon juice and cook for 20 to 30 minutes or until tender. Drain and cut in cubes into a bowl. Add remaining lemon juice and set aside to cool. Add 3 diced hard-cooked eggs, onion, parsley, pepper and mayonnaise. Taste and add salt, if desired. Mix well and turn into a serving bowl. Garnish with slices of hard-cooked egg and olives and sprinkle with paprika. Chill for at least 1 hour, before serving. 6 to 8 servings.

Mrs. Marian Finch, College Park, Georgia

Stuffed Artichokes (page 129)

WHIPPED CELERIAC

2 lge. celery roots	1/2 tsp. salt
1 lge. potato	1/4 tsp. pepper
1/4 to 1/2 c. chicken broth	Paprika
2 tbsp. butter	

Peel and quarter the celery roots and the potato. Cook the celery roots in boiling salted water until partially tender, then add the potato quarters. Continue cooking until vegetables are tender and drain. Mash the vegetables thoroughly. Add enough chicken broth to make a soft consistency as for mashed potatoes. Add butter, salt and pepper and whip until fluffy. Sprinkle with paprika and serve hot. 6 servings.

Mrs. B. L. Hembree, Cullman, Alabama

CLASSIC ARTICHOKES

1/4 c. salad or olive oil	1 tsp. salt
2 tbsp. lemon juice	Dash of pepper
2 sm. bay leaves	4 lge. artichokes
1 clove of garlic, split	

Boil 6 quarts water with the oil, lemon juice, bay leaves, garlic, salt and pepper. Trim the stalks from base of artichokes and cut 1-inch slice from top of each. Remove discolored leaves and snip off spike ends of leaves. Wash the artichokes in cold water and drain. Tie each with twine to hold leaves in place. Place in boiling water and reduce heat. Simmer, covered, for 30 minutes or until base is soft. Drain well and remove twine. Serve with mayonnaise, tartar sauce or lemon butter. 4 servings.

Mrs. Helen Penny Hill, Turnersville, Texas

STUFFED ARTICHOKES

4 fresh artichokes	1/4 c. chopped fresh celery
Salt	2 slices crisp bacon, crumbled
1 6 1/2-oz. can sm. shrimp	1 tsp. horseradish
2 hard-boiled eggs, chopped	Sour cream

Wash the artichokes. Cut off stems at base and remove small bottom leaves. Trim the tips of leaves and cut off about 1 inch from top of artichokes. Stand artichokes upright in a deep saucepan large enough to hold snugly. Add 1 teaspoon salt and 2 to 3 inches of boiling water and cover. Cook over low heat for 35 to 45 minutes or until base may be pierced easily with a fork, adding boiling water, if needed. Turn artichokes upside down to drain. Spread leaves gently and remove choke from center of artichokes with a metal spoon. Chill. Drain the shrimp and rinse with cold water. Drain well. Add the eggs, celery, bacon, salt to taste, horseradish and enough sour cream to moisten. Spread leaves of artichoke apart and stuff with shrimp mixture. Place on a serving dish and garnish with carrot slices, mushrooms and zucchini sticks.

Artichokes with Spanish Cauliflower (below)

ARTICHOKES WITH SPANISH CAULIFLOWER

6 artichokes
2 1/2 tsp. salt
1 med. head cauliflower
3/4 c. olive or salad oil
1/3 c. vinegar
1 tsp. sugar
1/4 tsp. basil leaves

1/8 tsp. pepper
1 2-oz. can anchovy fillets, drained and diced
2 tbsp. capers
1/4 c. sliced pimento-stuffed olives

Wash the artichokes. Cut off stems at base and remove small bottom leaves. Trim tips of the leaves and cut off about 1 inch from top of artichokes. Stand artichokes upright in a deep saucepan large enough to hold snugly. Add 1 1/2 teaspoons salt and 2 to 3 inches boiling water and cover. Simmer for 35 to 45 minutes or until base may be pierced easily with a fork, adding more boiling water, if needed. Turn artichokes upside down to drain. Spread leaves gently and remove choke from center of artichokes with a metal spoon. Chill. Separate the cauliflower into flowerets. Cook in boiling, salted water for about 10 minutes or until crisp-tender, then drain thoroughly. Mix remaining salt with remaining ingredients. Pour over the cauliflower in a large bowl and toss lightly. Cover and chill for several hours or overnight. Drain the cauliflower and reserve dressing. Fill each artichoke with about 1/2 cup cauliflower and serve with reserved dressing.

ARTICHOKE HEARTS AND PECANS

2 No. 2 cans artichoke hearts, drained
2 tbsp. butter
2 tbsp. flour
1 c. sweet cream

Salt and pepper to taste
Hot sauce to taste
1/2 c. broken pecans
1/4 c. bread crumbs
2 tbsp. Parmesan cheese

Stand the artichoke hearts in a small casserole. Melt the butter in a saucepan and blend in the flour. Add the cream gradually. Cook until thickened, stirring constantly. Season with salt, pepper and hot sauce. Pour the sauce into the casserole and add the pecans. Sprinkle with the bread crumbs and cheese. Bake at 300 degrees until bubbly. 6 servings.

Betty Cauthen, Charlotte, North Carolina

ARTICHOKE HEARTS IN LEMON BUTTER

1/2 c. minced onion	3 tbsp. lemon juice
1/2 clove of garlic, crushed	1 1/2 tsp. salt
2 tbsp. butter	1 tsp. oregano
3/4 c. chicken broth	1/4 tsp. grated lemon rind
2 15-oz. cans artichoke hearts	

Saute the onion and garlic in butter until transparent, then add the broth and artichoke hearts. Season with the lemon juice, salt, oregano and lemon rind. Simmer over low heat for 10 minutes or until artichokes are heated through. 6-8 servings.

Florence B. Fisackerly, Inverness, Mississippi

ARTICHOKE HEARTS ELEGANTE

1 pkg. frozen artichokes	1 tsp. salt
1 tbsp. dried minced onion	Freshly ground pepper
1 clove of garlic, crushed	1/4 c. olive oil
1 tbsp. chopped parsley	2 tbsp. water
1/2 c. dry bread crumbs	4 tbsp. Parmesan cheese

Cook the artichokes in boiling salted water for 5 minutes and drain well. Place in a buttered baking dish. Mix all remaining ingredients and sprinkle over the artichokes. Bake at 400 degrees for 20 minutes or until soft. 4 servings.

Mrs. Robert Still, Lexington, Kentucky

ARTICHOKE CASSEROLE SUPREME

12 artichokes	1/4 c. lemon juice
1 tsp. salt	Chopped cooked seafood
1 clove of garlic, crushed	1 recipe med. white sauce
1 tbsp. salad oil	

Break off the stems from artichokes to about 1/2 inch and remove the outer leaves and thorny leaf tips. Tie with string to keep leaves in place. Combine 1 cup boiling salted water, garlic, salad oil and lemon juice. Pour over artichokes in a saucepan. Cook, covered, for 30 minutes. Remove carefully and trim stems. Place the artichokes in a baking dish, then spoon the seafood and white sauce over the artichokes. Bake at 350 degrees for 20 minutes.

Mrs. Kelley Storey, Paris, Texas

Split Artichokes with Pate Dip (below)

SPLIT ARTICHOKES WITH PATE DIP

3 artichokes	6 cherry tomatoes, chilled
4 1/2 tsp. lemon juice	1/2 c. sour cream
3/4 tsp. salt	1 c. mayonnaise
12 cooked shelled shrimp,	2 tsp. prepared mustard
deveined	1 tbsp. chopped chives
1/4 c. canned liver pate	

Wash the artichokes and trim stems to 1 inch. Pull off tough outer leaves and snip off tips of remaining leaves. Place artichokes in 1 inch boiling water and add lemon juice. Sprinkle each artichoke with 1/4 teaspoon salt and cover tightly. Cook over low heat for 20 to 45 minutes depending upon size of artichokes or until stems may be pierced easily with a fork. Turn artichokes upside down to drain, then chill. Chill the shrimp and liver pate. Cut artichokes into halves and remove chokes with a small, sharp knife. Place 2 shrimp and 1 cherry tomato in the center of each artichoke half. Combine the sour cream, mayonnaise, mustard, liver pate and chives and blend until smooth. Serve with artichokes. 6 servings.

SHRIMP AND ARTICHOKE CASSEROLE

1 10-oz. package frozen artichoke	1 can cream of mushroom soup
hearts	1/4 c. grated Parmesan cheese
3/4 lb. cooked shrimp	1/2 tsp. salt
1/4 lb. fresh mushrooms, sliced	1/4 tsp. pepper
2 tbsp. butter	Paprika
1 tbsp. Worcestershire sauce	Parsley
1/4 c. dry sherry	

Arrange the artichoke hearts in a buttered baking dish. Arrange the shrimp and mushrooms over the artichokes and dot with butter. Mix Worcestershire sauce and the sherry with the soup; pour over the ingredients in the baking dish. Sprinkle with the cheese, salt, pepper and paprika. Bake at 375 degrees for 30 to 40 minutes. Garnish with parsley. 4-6 servings.

Mrs. Forbes S. Hascall, Tallahassee, Florida

STUFFED ARTICHOKES

4 med. artichokes	1 tsp. salt
2/3 c. fine dry bread crumbs	3/4 tsp. pepper
1 tsp. grated cheese	2 c. water
Chopped parsley	2 tbsp. olive oil

Remove the outside lower leaves from the artichokes and cut off the stems. Cover with cold salted water and let stand for 20 to 30 minutes. Blend the bread crumbs, cheese, 1 teaspoon parsley, salt and pepper. Wash the artichokes and spread open the leaves. Place the bread crumb mixture between the leaves. Stand artichokes in skillet and add water, 1 tablespoon parsley and olive oil. Cook, covered, for 30 minutes or until tender. Pull out leaves, one by one, to eat.

Sister M. Joanna, DM, Meridian, Mississippi

ARTICHOKE HEARTS WITH ONIONS

6 lge. artichokes	1/2 c. olive oil
Juice of 1 lemon	Salt to taste
6 lge. onions, thinly sliced	3/4 tsp. monosodium glutamate

Remove the stems from the artichokes and peel off tough outer leaves. Lay each one on its side and cut off an inch or more of the tops so that only the very tender portion of leaves remains. Halve lengthwise and remove the choke portion. Mix about 4 cups of water with half the lemon juice. Drop each artichoke into the water to prevent discoloration. Saute the onions in the oil, then place the artichoke halves cut side down on the onions. Add 1/2 cup water and remaining lemon juice and sprinkle with salt and monosodium glutamate. Simmer, covered, for about 45 minutes or until tender. Serve cold as an accompaniment or appetizer. 6 servings.

Mrs. Mildred Callahan, Miami, Florida

BOILED CARDOONS

1 bunch cardoons	1 tbsp. melted butter
1 tbsp. lemon juice or vinegar	

Wash and cut away hard outer stems and then cut into short pieces leaving the root or heart whole. Place in boiling salted water to cover. Add the lemon juice and cook for 1 hour and 30 minutes to 2 hours or until tender, adding water as needed. Serve with melted butter or hollandaise sauce.

Mrs. James Skinner, Dothan, Alabama

CARDOONS WITH PARMESAN SAUCE

4 c. cooked cardoons	1 sm. can tomato sauce
1 can beef bouillon	Parmesan cheese

Place the cardoons in layers in a casserole. Combine the bouillon and tomato sauce and thin with 1 sauce can water, if desired. Pour the sauce over the cardoons and sprinkle with cheese. Bake in 350-degree oven until sauce bubbles.

Mrs. C. A. Williams, Austin, Texas

ITALIAN-FRIED CARDOONS

1/2 c. flour	Dash of cayenne
1 tsp. baking powder	3 eggs, well beaten
1/2 tsp. salt	2 tbsp. olive oil
1/8 tsp. white pepper	1 1-lb. bunch cardoons
Dash of nutmeg	Ripe black olives

Sift the flour, baking powder, salt, pepper, nutmeg and cayenne into a bowl. Make a well in the center and stir in eggs and olive oil gradually. Whip with wire whisk or egg beater until thoroughly blended and smooth. Cover and set aside. Wash and dry the cardoons. Strip prickles from stalks and cut into 3-inch lengths. Cover with boiling salted water and cook for about 15 minutes. Drain and rub off outer skin. Beat the batter again until light and creamy. Dip pieces of cardoon in batter. Fry in 375-degree oil for 3 to 5 minutes, until puffed and brown. Serve on a platter garnished with black ripe olives.

Mrs. Joe Rumore, Jackson, Mississippi

CARDOON RICHIRELLI

1 1-lb. bunch cardoons	1/4 tsp. pepper
1 1/2 c. bread crumbs	1 tsp. chopped parsley
4 tbsp. grated Parmesan cheese	2 eggs, lightly beaten
1/2 tsp. salt	1/4 c. flour

Wash and dry the cardoons. Strip prickles from stalks and cut the cardoons into 3-inch pieces. Cover with boiling salted water and boil over low heat for 12 minutes. Drain well and rub off outer skin with a cloth. Combine the bread crumbs, cheese, salt, pepper and parsley. Roll the cardoon pieces in the bread crumb mixture, then dip in beaten eggs. Dust lightly with flour and fry in 375-degree fat until golden brown.

Tomato Sauce

1 clove of garlic	2 c. stewed tomatoes, strained
3 tbsp. olive oil	Salt and pepper
1 onion, chopped	1/2 bay leaf
1/2 c. tomato paste	1/2 tsp. dill

Cook the garlic in the olive oil for 3 minutes, then discard. Add the onion and cook until tender. Stir in the tomato paste, strained tomatoes, 1 cup water, salt, pepper, bay leaf and dill and cook until quite thick. Serve with the fried cardoons.

Maria Tomaselli, Takoma Park, Maryland

BREADED DANDELION BLOSSOMS

1/4 c. milk	1/2 c. flour
2 tbsp. powdered milk	Pinch of salt
1 tbsp. baking powder	16 lge. fresh dandelion blossoms
1 egg	Fat

Mix all ingredients except dandelion blossoms and fat. Wash the blossoms lightly and drain. Do not allow to wilt. Dip the blossoms into batter and fry in deep fat until golden. 4 servings.

Elizabeth Skaggs, Birmingham, Alabama

SPICED FIDDLEHEADS

2 qt. fiddleheads	2 stalks celery, chopped
Juice of 1 lemon	1 stalk fennel, chopped
1/2 c. salad oil	1/4 tsp. coriander seed
3 tbsp. vinegar	Peppercorns
1 tsp. salt	

Trim the stem ends from the fiddleheads and discard. Wash the fiddleheads thoroughly. Combine the lemon juice, 3 cups water, the salad oil, vinegar, salt, celery, fennel, coriander seed and several peppercorns in a saucepan and bring to a boil. Add the fiddleheads and cook over low heat for 15 to 25 minutes. Serve cool.

Mrs. Sara Birch, Summersville, West Virginia

FIDDLEHEADS

1 can fiddleheads	Salt to taste
Bread slices	Chopped onion
Soft sweet butter	Mayonnaise

Drain the fiddleheads well. Cut the bread into small rounds and spread with butter. Place 1 fiddlehead on each round, then add a dash of salt and small amount of chopped onion. Top with a small dab of mayonnaise. 4-6 servings.

Mrs. Robert W. Higbie, Jr., New Orleans, Louisiana

FAVORITE STUFFED VEGETABLE PEARS

3 vegetable pears
1 lb. ground beef
2 med. onions, chopped
2 garlic cloves, minced

2 tbsp. cooking oil
2 c. water
3 to 4 slices toast
2 eggs, beaten

Boil whole pears until tender. Cut in half lengthwise and remove flat seed. Scoop out the centers, leaving shell. Fry the ground beef, onions and garlic in oil over low heat until light brown, stirring frequently. Add the water and cook for about 10 minutes. Remove from heat. Soften the toast in a small amount of water and break into pieces. Add the vegetable pear pulp and toast to ground beef mixture and stir in eggs. Fill the pear shells. Cover with additional toast crumbs. Place in a flat pan with small amount of water covering bottom. Bake in 350-degree oven for 15 to 20 minutes or until lightly browned. Serve hot or cold. 6 servings.

Dorothy Greenlaw Marguart, Franklinton, Louisiana

STUFFED MIRLITONS

4 young tender mirlitons
1 lge. onion, minced
1/2 stick margarine

1 pkg. frozen shrimp
Salt and pepper to taste
Italian-flavored bread crumbs

Boil unpeeled whole mirlitons for about 45 minutes or until tender. Drain and allow to cool enough to handle. Split down middle, following natural crevices. Remove seed and fiber with a spoon. Scrape out tender meat of mirliton, leaving about 1/8-inch meat on shell for stuffing. Saute the onion in margarine until slightly browned. Peel the shrimp, then chop and add to the onion. Saute the shrimp mixture for 10 minutes over low heat. Add the mirliton meat and cook for 10 minutes longer. Mixture will be soupy if mirlitons are young and juicy. Season with salt and pepper. Add enough bread crumbs to absorb moisture and give consistency of a stuffing. Pile into mirliton shells and top with crumbs. Bake for 20 minutes at 350 degrees.

Mrs. Seeman Glasscock, Sr., Opelousas, Louisiana

BRUSSELS SPROUTS WITH CHESTNUTS

2 tbsp. butter
2 tsp. flour
1/4 tsp. salt
Pinch of white pepper
1/4 tsp. basil

3/4 c. chicken broth
3 lb. fresh Brussels sprouts
1 1/2 c. peeled, sliced cooked
   chestnuts

Melt the butter in a saucepan and add the flour, salt, pepper and basil. Stir in the chicken broth. Cook the mixture until slightly thickened. Keep warm over simmering water. Cook the Brussels sprouts in boiling salted water until crisp but tender. Drain thoroughly. Place the Brussels sprouts in a serving dish. Add the chestnuts to the cream sauce, then pour sauce over the Brussels sprouts. Three packages frozen Brussels sprouts may be substituted for the fresh Brussels sprouts. Cook according to package directions. 8 servings.

Harriet Troy, Louisville, Kentucky

BRUSSELS SPROUTS IN CELERY SAUCE

2 qt. Brussels sprouts	6 tbsp. flour
1 1/8 tsp. salt	Milk
1 1/2 c. diced celery	Dash of pepper
6 tbsp. butter	

Remove wilted Brussels sprouts leaves and wash. Cook the Brussels sprouts until tender and drain. Combine salt, 2 1/4 cups boiling water and celery in a sauce-pan and boil for 15 minutes. Drain, reserving the celery liquid. Melt the butter and blend in the flour. Combine the reserved liquid with enough milk to measure 3 cups. Stir milk mixture gradually into the flour mixture. Cook until smooth and thick, stirring constantly. Add the celery and pepper and pour over the Brussels sprouts. 8 servings.

Mrs. Margaret Cepelka, Berryville, Virginia

CHOUX DE BRUXELLES VERONIQUE

1 1/2 c. chicken stock	2 tbsp. butter or margarine
3 10-oz. packages frozen	1/2 c. dry white wine
California Brussels sprouts	Dash of white pepper
1 c. seedless white grapes	

Bring the stock to a boil in a large saucepan or chafing dish. Add the Brussels sprouts and cover. Cook over low heat for 5 to 10 minutes or until almost tender. Stir in the grapes, butter, wine and pepper and cook for 5 to 7 minutes longer. Drain and serve with roast fowl and game birds, if desired. Drained liquid may be used for flavoring soups or sauces.

Choux de Bruxelles Veronique (above)

Cavoli di Brussele alla Romano (below)

CAVOLI DI BRUSSELE ALLA ROMANO

3 onion bouillon cubes
2 1/2 c. boiling water
1 1/2 tbsp. olive or
   salad oil
1 tbsp. anchovy paste

4 10-oz. packages frozen
   California Brussels sprouts
1/3 c. sliced ripe olives
2 tbsp. pine nuts
3 tbsp. dry white wine

Combine the bouillon cubes, water, oil and anchovy paste in a saucepan and cook, stirring, until bouillon cubes dissolve. Add the Brussels sprouts and cover. Cook for 5 minutes or until Brussels sprouts are almost tender. Mix in the olives, pine nuts and wine and cook over low heat until Brussels sprouts are just tender. 10-12 servings.

BRUSSELS SPROUTS WITH YAM FRILL

8 cooked yams
1/2 c. brown sugar
5 tbsp. butter, melted
3/4 c. orange juice
3 tbsp. grated orange peel

1/2 tsp. nutmeg
1/2 tsp. allspice
2 10-oz. packages frozen
   Brussels sprouts
1/4 tsp. white pepper

Peel and mash the yams until smooth. Blend the sugar, 2 tablespoons butter, 1/4 cup orange juice, 2 tablespoons orange peel, 1/4 teaspoon nutmeg and 1/8 teaspoon allspice into yams and whip until light and fluffy. Heat to serving temperature and keep hot. Cook the Brussels sprouts according to package directions, then drain. Toss gently with remaining butter, orange juice and peel, nutmeg, allspice and white pepper. Cook over low heat. Place the Brussels sprouts in the center of a large platter and spoon the whipped potatoes around the edge. 6-8 servings.

Mrs. Ouida Anderson, Ellicott City, Maryland

BRUSSELS SPROUTS WITH GRAPES

2 pkg. frozen Brussels sprouts	1 tsp. sugar
3/4 c. sour cream	1/2 tsp. pepper
1/2 c. slivered almonds	2 tsp. salt
2/3 c. drained mushrooms	3/4 c. grated American cheese
1 c. seedless white grapes	Paprika
1/4 c. chopped pimento	

Cook the Brussels sprouts according to package directions and drain. Add the sour cream, almonds, mushrooms, grapes, pimento, sugar and seasonings. Heat in a double boiler for 7 minutes. Place in a serving dish and sprinkle with the cheese and paprika. 8-10 servings.

Novella Mae Melton, Roswell, New Mexico

FRIED SALSIFY STICKS

1 1/2 lb. salsify	1 c. flour
1 tsp. vinegar	2/3 c. milk
Salt	2 eggs, beaten
2 peppercorns	

Peel the salsify and cut in 3-inch lengths. Place in cold water to cover and add the vinegar to prevent discoloration. Add 1/2 teaspoon salt and the peppercorns. Bring to a boil and cook until the salsify is slightly tender. Remove the peppercorns. Drain the salsify and dry with paper towels. Sift the flour and 1/2 teaspoon salt together. Combine the milk and eggs and add to the flour. Heat the deep fat to 375 degrees. Place several pieces of salsify in the batter at a time and drop, 1 at a time, into the hot fat. Cook until brown and lift out. Drain on paper towels and place on ovenproof platter. Keep hot in warm oven.

Mrs. Marie Morgan, Eclectic, Alabama

SAVORY SALSIFY CASSEROLE

4 c. sliced salsify	1 can oyster stew
1 tsp. vinegar	1 c. coarse cracker crumbs
Salt to taste	Pepper to taste
2 eggs, beaten	1 tbsp. butter or margarine
1 6-oz. can evaporated milk	1/8 tsp. paprika

Soak the salsify in cold water and vinegar and drain. Cover with water and bring to a boil. Add 1/2 teaspoon salt and cook for about 15 minutes or until tender. Drain and allow to cool. Combine the eggs, milk and oyster stew. Place the salsify in a casserole and pour the oyster stew over it. Add the crumbs and fold into the oyster stew and salsify. Season with salt and pepper. Dot with butter and sprinkle with paprika. Bake at 350 degrees for about 45 minutes or until set. 6-8 servings.

Mrs. Harlan Dixon, Hyden, Kentucky

SALSIFY PATTIES

4 c. chopped salsify	4 tbsp. butter or margarine
1 tsp. vinegar	1/8 tsp. garlic powder
1/2 tsp. salt	Flour
1/8 tsp. pepper	

Drop the salsify in cold water to cover and add vinegar and salt. Bring to a boil and cook, covered, for 15 to 20 minutes or until tender enough to mash. Drain thoroughly. Mash the salsify, adding pepper, 1 tablespoon butter and garlic powder. Form in flat patties about 3 inches in diameter. Dredge lightly with flour. Cook in remaining butter. 12 patties or 6 servings.

Mrs. S. E. Anderson, Jamestown, Tennessee

SALSIFY WITH HERB SAUCE

1 1/2 lb. salsify	1 tsp. chopped chives
1 tsp. vinegar	1/2 tsp. dillweed
Salt	Flour
4 tbsp. butter or margarine	1 tbsp. lemon juice
2 tsp. chopped parsley	

Wash the salsify and peel as thinly as possible. Cut in 1-inch lengths. Cover with cold water and add the vinegar and 1/2 teaspoon salt. Bring to a boil. Cook, covered, for 15 to 20 minutes, until just tender and drain. Melt the butter and add the parsley, chives, dillweed and 1/2 teaspoon salt. Keep warm over low heat. Dredge the salsify pieces with flour. Add to butter and cook until light brown. Add lemon juice just before serving. Serve with the herb sauce. 6 servings.

Mrs. Eva Thomas, Decatur, Georgia

BUFFET SALSIFY

1 1/2 lb. salsify	Butter
1 tsp. vinegar	3 tbsp. flour
1/2 tsp. salt	1 1/2 c. milk
1/4 tsp. celery salt	1/2 c. bread crumbs
Dash of white pepper	Dash of paprika
1 egg, beaten	

Wash and chop the salsify. Cover with cold water in a saucepan and add the vinegar and salt. Add the celery salt and pepper. Bring to a boil and cook, covered, for 15 to 20 minutes or until tender. Drain thoroughly and mash. Add the egg and stir briskly until well mixed. Melt 3 tablespoons butter in a saucepan and add the flour, stirring until smooth. Add the milk gradually. Cook and stir over low heat until smooth and thick. Stir in the mashed salsify mixture. Lightly grease 6 individual casseroles and place on a baking sheet. Turn salsify mixture into casseroles. Heat the crumbs in 2 tablespoons butter, then sprinkle the crumbs and paprika over the salsify. Place under broiler to brown the crumbs. 6 servings.

Mrs. Virginia London, Covington, Kentucky

FRIED PUMPKIN BLOOMS

16 fresh pumpkin blooms   Fine cracker crumbs
1 or 2 eggs, well beaten   Salt and pepper to taste

Blooms must be cut in early morning before closing. Divide in half and wash, then place in salt water until ready to use. Remove from water and dip in eggs, then roll in crumbs. Place in a well-greased skillet. Cook at low temperature until golden brown. Season. Serve while hot. 4 servings.

Kay Mathias, Roanoke, Virginia

OYSTER PLANT CASSEROLE

12 oyster plants, sliced   1/2 tsp. pepper
6 plain crackers, crumbled   1 tbsp. margarine
1/2 tsp. salt   1 1/2 c. milk

Place the oyster plants and crackers in alternate layers in a casserole until all have been used. Mix remaining ingredients and pour over the top. Bake at 350 degrees about 30 minutes. 4 servings.

Louise Hunt, Kevil, Kentucky

SAUTEED TRUFFLES

1/2 lb. truffles   2 tbsp. white wine
1 garlic clove   1 tbsp. brandy
3 tbsp. olive oil   Salt and pepper to taste
Juice of 1/2 lemon

Wash the truffles in several changes of water. Scrub with a brush to clean thoroughly. Rub a sharp knife with the garlic, then cut the truffles into 1/4-inch slices. Place the garlic, olive oil, lemon juice, wine, brandy, salt and pepper in a heatproof casserole and bring to a boil. Add the truffles and saute, but do not overcook.

Mrs. Susan Wyatt, Valley Station, Kentucky

TRUFFLE STUFFING

6 to 8 fresh truffles   4 tbsp. cognac
1 1/2 c. goose liver   6 tbsp. Madeira
2 tbsp. meat extract

Cut large truffles in half and cut the goose liver in large pieces. Combine the truffles, goose liver and meat extract and moisten with the cognac and Madeira. Stuffing may be used for game birds.

Mrs. Patricia Renaud, Huntington, West Virginia

MUSHROOMS BAKED IN CREAM

1 lb. mushrooms
2 tsp. minced onion
1/3 c. butter or margarine
1/4 tsp. pepper
1/4 tsp. monosodium glutamate
1/4 tsp. salt

1/4 tsp. paprika
1/3 c. toasted bread crumbs
3 slices bacon, crumbled
1/2 tsp. Worcestershire sauce
1 c. cream

Wash the mushrooms and remove the stems from the caps. Reserve the caps and finely chop the stems. Cook the stems and onion in butter over low heat until tender. Blend pepper, monosodium glutamate, salt, paprika and bread crumbs with onions and mushroom stems. Arrange the mushroom caps in a shallow greased casserole. Fill with the bread crumb mixture and top with bacon. Mix Worcestershire sauce and cream and pour around the mushrooms. Bake at 375 degrees for 15 minutes.

Mrs. Nancy Carter, Fayetteville, Arkansas

MUSHROOM FONDUE

1 lb. fresh mushrooms
1 c. finely chopped celery
2/3 c. margarine
8 eggs, beaten

1 1/3 c. milk
5 c. soft bread crumbs
1 tbsp. chopped pimento
2 tsp. salt

Finely chop the mushrooms and saute with celery in margarine. Blend the eggs, milk, bread crumbs, pimento and salt. Fold in sauteed vegetables. Pour into 2-quart buttered ring mold and set the mold in a pan of hot water. Bake at 350 degrees for 40 minutes. Turn onto hot serving dish. Center may be filled with cream sauce. 8 servings.

Mrs. Carolyn Fillmore Frederick, Jackson, Mississippi

GOURMET STUFFED MUSHROOMS

1 lb. medium fresh mushrooms
1 tbsp. butter or margarine
3/4 c. finely chopped onions
Salad oil
Seasoned salt
3 slices bread
1 tbsp. parsley flakes
1/2 tsp. salt

1/8 tsp. pepper
1/4 tsp. marjoram
1/4 tsp. thyme
1 tsp. Worcestershire sauce
3 tbsp. bouillon
1 egg, slightly beaten
1/4 c. toasted slivered almonds

Wash and stem the mushrooms and dry on paper towels. Chop stems fine. Melt the butter in a saucepan and add stems and onions. Saute until onions are transparent. Brush the mushroom caps with oil and arrange, hollow side up, in a shallow baking dish. Sprinkle with seasoned salt. Remove the crusts from the bread and cut in cubes. Remove sauteed mixture from heat and add bread cubes and remaining ingredients. Fill the caps with the stuffing. Bake at 425 degrees for about 15 minutes or until mushrooms are tender but not limp. 6-10 servings.

Mrs. Virginia Mullen, Louisville, Kentucky

CARAWAY-CREAMED MUSHROOMS

1 lb. fresh mushrooms, sliced	1 tsp. salt
1/2 c. thinly sliced onions	1/8 tsp. pepper
2 tsp. caraway seed	1 tall can evaporated milk
1/3 c. butter	1 tbsp. lemon juice
3 tbsp. flour	

Saute the mushrooms, onions and caraway seed in butter in a saucepan over low heat until onions are tender, then remove from heat. Stir in the flour, salt and pepper. Stir in undiluted evaporated milk slowly and cook over medium heat, stirring occasionally, until thickened. Stir in the lemon juice just before serving. Serve over waffles, toast or in patty shells. 6 servings.

Caraway-Creamed Mushrooms (above)

Marinated Mushrooms (below)

MARINATED MUSHROOMS

1 lb. fresh mushrooms	1/4 tsp. dried leaf oregano
6 tbsp. olive oil	1/4 c. chopped fresh parsley
3/4 c. dry white wine	2 tbsp. chopped fresh onion
1 1/2 tsp. salt	3 tbsp. fresh lemon juice
1/8 tsp. cayenne pepper	

Slice the mushrooms and place in a glass or earthenware bowl. Combine remaining ingredients in a saucepan and simmer for 15 minutes. Remove from heat and pour over mushrooms. Cover and refrigerate for several hours. 8 servings.

MUSHROOM DELIGHT

3/4 lb. small fresh mushrooms	1/2 tsp. sugar
6 tbsp. olive oil	1/4 tsp. pepper
3 tbsp. white vinegar	1/4 c. finely chopped onion
1 tsp. oregano leaves	2 tbsp. diced pimento
1 tsp. salt	1/2 clove of garlic, minced

Rinse, pat dry and trim stems from fresh mushrooms. Cover with boiling water and let set for 1 minute. Drain. Immerse in ice water until completely chilled, then drain thoroughly. Combine the oil, vinegar, oregano, salt, sugar and pepper in a small bowl and mix well. Stir in the onion, pimento and garlic. Place alternate layers of mushrooms and vinegar mixture in a quart jar and cover. Chill thoroughly. Serve as an appetizer or side dish. The mushrooms keep for several weeks in refrigerator. Two 6 or 8-ounce cans whole mushrooms, drained, may be substituted for fresh mushrooms. 1 quart.

BAKED MUSHROOM-STUFFED TOMATOES

6 fresh tomatoes	2 tbsp. melted butter or
Salt	margarine
6 lge. fresh mushrooms	

Preheat oven to 350 degrees. Cut a slice from top of each tomato and scoop out some of the pulp carefully. Sprinkle lightly with salt. Remove stems from the mushrooms and place 1 in each tomato, cavity side up. Brush with butter. Arrange tomatoes in a buttered casserole and cover with foil. Bake for 35 to 40 minutes or until done. Sprinkle with chopped parsley, if desired. 6 servings.

Photograph for this recipe on page 126.

MUSHROOMS MAGNIFIQUE

12 lge. mushrooms, cleaned	1 1/2 tbsp. chopped parsley
Salt	1/2 clove of garlic, minced
2 tbsp. softened butter	1/8 tsp. thyme
1/2 c. finely chopped pecans	1/2 c. heavy cream

Remove the stems from the mushrooms and finely chop enough stems to measure 1/4 cup. Salt the caps lightly. Blend the butter with stems, pecans, parsley, garlic, 1/4 teaspoon salt and thyme and stuff the mushroom caps. Place the caps in a shallow baking pan and cover with cream. Bake at 350 degrees for 20 minutes, basting occasionally with additional cream. 6 servings.

Mrs. Florence Smith, Little Rock, Arkansas

MUSHROOMS WITH BACON

2 lb. fresh mushrooms	1 tsp. salt
1/2 stick butter	1/2 tsp. pepper
1 med. onion, chopped	1 tbsp. minced parsley
1 tbsp. flour	3 strips cooked bacon,
1 c. sour cream	crumbled

Wash the mushrooms and cut off stems. Slice the caps in quarters, if large. Saute in butter in a saucepan for several minutes. Add the onion and cover. Cook over low heat for 15 minutes. Sprinkle with flour and stir lightly. Add the sour cream, salt and pepper and heat through. Do not boil. Sprinkle with parsley and bacon and serve at once. Three green onions may be substituted for onion. 6 servings.

Mrs. Elizabeth L. Jeffries, Johnson City, Tennessee

Holiday Vegetable Medley (page 150)

mixed vegetables

Individual vegetables, properly cooked and seasoned with a light touch, add so much to the meal. Mixing those vegetables not only brings extra flavor interest to a meal, but also provides today's cost-conscious homemakers an opportunity to make the most of leftovers!

Southern homemakers have mixed and matched vegetables in many unusual dishes certain to bring compliments from your family. Picture, for instance, how Artichokes and Spinach with Hollandaise Sauce will be received at your dinner table. And, if you really want to taste vegetables at their southern best, prepare Tomato-Okra Pilau, a dish originally developed in South Carolina's kitchens. This rice-based concoction is hearty enough to serve as your main dish — and its rich blending of vegetable flavors will remain a delicious memory!

Tomato blends well with other vegetables, too — as in Fresh Corn and Tomato Casserole. Corn plays a role in Indian Summer Succotash, which combines several favorite vegetables of the earliest Americans into a dish which every southern colonist learned to enjoy.

This section is packed with such recipes. Every one is the home-tested favorite of the woman who shares it with you. These recipes combine the flavor, color, and texture of different vegetables in one dish . . . and bring new interest and zing to your table!

ASPARAGUS AND CARROTS

1 lb. cooked asparagus
2 c. sliced cooked carrots
2 1/2 tbsp. butter
2 tbsp. flour

1 c. hot milk
Salt to taste
1 slice bread, toasted

Drain the asparagus and combine with the carrots in a baking dish. Melt the butter in a saucepan and stir in the flour. Add the milk gradually, stirring until smooth. Bring to a boil and add the salt. Pour the sauce over the vegetables and mix well. Crumble the toast over the vegetable mixture. Additional toast crumbs may be used if the sauce is thinner than desired.

Mrs. M. R. Lovett, Williamsburg, Kentucky

ASPARAGUS AND ENGLISH PEA CASSEROLE

1 10-oz. package frozen
   English peas
1 10-oz. can cut asparagus
1 sm. can sliced mushrooms
Butter

1 1/2 tbsp. flour
1/2 c. milk
2/3 c. grated Velveeta cheese
Salt and pepper to taste
1 c. cracker crumbs

Cook the peas according to package directions. Drain and reserve liquid. Drain the asparagus and mushrooms and reserve liquids. Mix all reserved liquids in a saucepan and boil until reduced to 1/2 cup. Melt 2 tablespoons butter in a saucepan and stir in flour. Add the milk and vegetable liquid and cook, stirring constantly, until thickened. Add the cheese, salt and pepper and stir until cheese is melted. Remove from heat. Place the peas, asparagus and mushrooms in a casserole and cover with cheese sauce. Mix gently. Top with cracker crumbs and dot generously with butter. Bake at 325 degrees for 20 minutes or until lightly browned. 6 servings.

Mrs. William H. Hughes, Nashville, Arkansas

ARTICHOKES AND SPINACH WITH HOLLANDAISE SAUCE

2 pkg. frozen spinach
1 1-lb. can artichoke hearts
2 egg yolks

3 tbsp. lemon juice
1/2 c. butter

Cook the spinach according to package directions and drain well. Arrange the artichoke hearts in a buttered baking dish. Heap each heart with spinach. Mix the egg yolks and lemon juice in the top of a double boiler and cook over low heat. Add 1/4 cup butter and cook and stir until melted. Add remaining butter and cook, stirring constantly, until the sauce is thickened. Pour the sauce over the artichokes. Bake at 250 degrees until heated through. 6-8 servings.

Mrs. Richard E. Boquist, Dover, Delaware

BAKED GREEN BEANS AND MUSHROOMS

4 c. bread cubes
1/2 c. melted margarine
2 cans cut green beans,
   drained
2 cans sliced mushrooms,
   drained

Salt and pepper to taste
1 sm. onion, diced
1 can cream of mushroom soup
1/3 soup can milk
1/4 c. toasted slivered
   almonds (opt.)

Preheat oven to 400 degrees. Toss the bread cubes with margarine and place half the bread cubes in a greased 2-quart casserole. Cover with beans and top with mushrooms. Sprinkle with salt, pepper and onion. Combine the soup and milk and mix well. Pour over onion. Top with remaining bread cubes and almonds. Bake for 30 minutes. 8 servings.

Mrs. F. T. Murphy, Sarasota, Florida

GREEN BEAN CASSEROLE

2 cans seasoned green beans
2 pkg. frozen lima beans
2 pkg. frozen green peas
1 1/4 c. mayonnaise
1 tsp. Worcestershire sauce

1 tsp. mustard
Juice of 1 lemon
Dash of garlic salt
Dash of hot sauce
1 med. onion, grated

Drain the green beans. Cook the frozen beans and peas according to package directions and drain. Combine the vegetables in a heatproof casserole. Mix the remaining ingredients and stir into the green bean mixture. Cook over medium heat until all the ingredients are heated through.

Mrs. L. E. Terry, Cookeville, Tennessee

VEGETABLE CASSEROLE

3 slices bacon
3 c. cut cabbage
Salt and pepper
3 c. sliced tender squash

Butter or margarine
1 c. onion rings
1 can cream of mushroom soup

Fry the bacon until crisp, then remove from the pan and reserve. Add the cabbage to the bacon fat and add salt and pepper to taste. Cook and stir until transparent. Cook the squash in a small amount of water for 6 to 7 minutes. Add a dash of salt and 1 tablespoon butter. Cook and stir the onion rings in a small amount of butter for about 5 minutes or until clear, but not brown. Crumble reserved bacon over the cabbage and mix. Place a layer of cabbage in a buttered casserole and top with the onions, then the squash. Repeat until all are used. Pour the soup and 2 tablespoons water over the top and cover. Bake at 375 to 400 degrees for 20 minutes.

Mrs. R. O. Munden, Carthage, Texas

Cranberry-Braised Endive and Mushrooms (below)

CRANBERRY-BRAISED ENDIVE AND MUSHROOMS

1 lb. fresh mushrooms	1/2 c. white wine
1/2 c. butter or margarine	1/2 c. cranberry-orange relish
6 endive	

Slice the mushrooms if large. Melt the butter in a large skillet. Trim the endive and cut into halves. Add to skillet. Add the mushrooms and saute until lightly browned. Add the wine and cover. Simmer for about 20 minutes or until tender. Stir in the cranberry-orange relish and heat to serving temperature. Six stalks celery, cut into 4-inch long strips, may be substituted for endive. 6 servings.

HOLIDAY VEGETABLE MEDLEY

1/2 lb. fresh mushrooms	4 tsp. cornstarch
1 15 1/2-oz. can sm. whole	1/4 tsp. ground nutmeg
peeled onions	1 9-oz. package frozen whole
1/2 c. skim milk	green beans

Rinse, pat dry and slice the fresh mushrooms and set aside. Drain the onions and reserve liquid. Combine reserved liquid, skim milk, cornstarch and nutmeg in a saucepan and bring to boiling point, stirring constantly. Reduce heat. Add the mushrooms and onions and simmer for 4 to 5 minutes, stirring occasionally. Cook the beans according to package directions, then drain. Place the mushroom mixture and sauce in a serving dish and surround with hot beans, spooning sauce over beans. Serve with meat or poultry, if desired. One 6 or 8-ounce can sliced mushrooms, drained, may be substituted for fresh mushrooms. 6 servings.

Photograph for this recipe on page 146.

CORN BREAD VEGETABLE SQUARES

1 sm. box corn bread mix	1 can cream of mushroom soup
1 No. 2 can mixed vegetables	2/3 c. water

Prepare the corn bread batter according to package instructions. Drain the vegetables, then fold into the corn bread batter. Pour into a well-greased 9-inch square pan. Bake at 375 degrees until done. Pour the soup in a saucepan and add the water gradually. Heat, stirring until smooth, then pour over the corn bread squares. 6 servings.

Mrs. Naomi Stock, Austin, Texas

VEGETABLES IN CHEESE SAUCE

1 c. diced cooked carrots	4 tbsp. flour
8 sm. onions, cooked	2 c. hot milk
1 1/2 c. canned cut green beans	1/2 lb. American cheese, diced
1 c. canned peas	1/2 tsp. salt
4 tbsp. butter or margarine	1 can refrigerator biscuits

Place the vegetables in a greased casserole. Melt the butter in a saucepan and blend in the flour. Add the milk slowly, and cook, stirring constantly until the sauce is thick, then add the cheese and salt. Stir until the cheese is melted and pour the sauce over the vegetables. Arrange the biscuits around edge of casserole. Bake at 425 degrees for 15 minutes.

Mrs. Johnny R. Mooring, Dallas, Texas

VEGETABLE LOAF

1/2 c. cooked peas	1 c. soft bread crumbs
1/2 c. chopped cooked string beans	1/2 tsp. salt
1/2 c. chopped cooked carrots	1/8 tsp. pepper
1 1/2 c. milk	1/2 tsp. paprika
1 egg, slightly beaten	

Press the peas through a sieve. Combine all the vegetables, then add remaining ingredients. Turn into a greased baking dish. Bake at 350 degrees until firm. 6 servings.

Nina D. Sonnier, Lake Charles, Louisiana

WHIPPED CARROTS AND POTATOES

3 lb. carrots	3 tbsp. light cream
Salt	1/2 pkg. instant mashed
1/8 tsp. pepper	potatoes

Scrape and chop the carrots, then cook with 3/4 teaspoon salt in boiling water until done and drain. Mash slightly and whip in 1/8 teaspoon salt, pepper and the cream. Prepare the potatoes according to package directions and whip into the carrots.

Mrs. Robert Barlow, Perryton, Texas

BEAN SALAD

1 can green beans	3/4 c. chopped celery
1 can wax beans	1 1/2 c. vinegar
1 can cut green beans	2/3 c. sugar
1 sm. onion, cut up	1/2 c. oil
1 bell pepper, cut up	

Drain the canned beans, then mix with the onion, pepper and celery. Mix the vinegar, sugar and oil together and pour over the bean mixture. Marinate for at least 24 hours before serving.

Evelyn Gore, Tabor City, North Carolina

CHAFING DISH VEGETABLES

1 lge. cauliflower	1 tsp. salt
1 lemon slice	1/8 tsp. pepper
2 tbsp. butter or margarine	1 tsp. chopped mint
1/2 lb. mushrooms	1 c. cooked peas, drained
1 1/2 c. light cream	

Cook the cauliflower in boiling water with lemon slice until tender but not mushy. Drain the cauliflower and separate into cauliflowerets. Melt butter in blazer pan over low heat. Add the mushrooms and brown. Add the cream, salt, pepper and mint. Place over hot water and heat until cream is warm. Add the peas and cauliflower and heat through. 6 servings.

Mrs. Al Keyes, Alexandria, Louisiana

MEAL IN A DISH

1 can sm. potatoes	6 pork sausage balls
1 sm. can English peas	1/2 c. milk
2 med. carrots, diced	2 tbsp. lard
2 c. water	Flour

Boil the vegetables in the water until carrots are about half done. Drop in the sausage and cook for 5 minutes. Combine milk, lard and enough flour to form a stiff dough. Roll thin and cut in strips. Drop the dumplings in the boiling mixture and cook for 5 minutes longer.

Mrs. Barney Herndon, Farmington, Kentucky

GREEN AND YELLOW CASSEROLE

1 can Blue Lake green beans	1 chopped pimento
1 can yellow whole corn	1 can mushroom soup
2 c. chopped carrots	1 tbsp. butter or margarine

Drain the beans and corn, then place a layer of each in a 2-quart casserole. Add a layer of carrots. Repeat layers. Mix the pimento with the soup and 3/4 cup water and pour over the vegetables. Add the butter. Bake at 350 degrees for 25 minutes.

Mrs. Helen Willis, Lignum, Virginia

OKRA-POTATO HASH

1 clove of garlic, scored
1 med. onion, diced
3 tbsp. fat or oil

1 lb. okra, sliced
2 med. potatoes, diced

Saute the garlic and onion in hot fat, then add the okra and potatoes. Cook until browned and cover. Cook until tender and remove the garlic. Serve hot. 4-5 servings.

Mrs. Ruby Maynard, Angleton, Texas

IMPERIAL GREEN PEAS

1 10-oz. package frozen green
   peas and celery
1 tbsp. butter
1/2 tsp. salt
1 1/2 c. boiling water

1 chicken bouillon cube
1/4 c. cold water
1 tbsp. cornstarch
1 5-oz. can water chestnuts

Add the peas and celery, butter and salt to 1/2 cup boiling water in a saucepan and cover. Cook over low heat for 2 to 3 minutes or until the peas and celery are tender-crisp. Remove from heat. Add the bouillon cube and stir until dissolved. Blend the cold water and cornstarch. Drain the water chestnuts and slice thin. Add the cornstarch mixture, remaining boiling water and the water chestnuts to peas and celery and cook just until thickened, stirring gently. About 4 servings.

Imperial Green Peas (above)

FRESH CORN AND TOMATO CASSEROLE

10 to 12 ears fresh corn	4 slices crisp bacon, crumbled
1/4 c. butter	1 tsp. salt
2 c. water	2 lge. tomatoes

Cut the corn from the cob to fill 4 to 5 cups. Melt the butter in a skillet, then add the corn. Saute quickly for about 5 minutes. Add the water, bacon and salt. Peel and slice the tomatoes. Arrange alternate layers of the corn mixture and tomato slices in a buttered baking dish. Bake at 350 degrees, uncovered, for about 30 minutes. Serve hot. 5-6 servings.

Mrs. Tom J. Groce, Albany, Kentucky

SCALLOPED TOMATOES AND CABBAGE

3 tbsp. shortening	1 tbsp. minced onion
1 1/4 c. dry bread crumbs	1/2 med. cabbage, coarsely
1 tsp. salt	shredded
1/4 tsp. celery salt	1 No. 2 can tomatoes
1/4 tsp. pepper	1/3 c. grated cheese

Melt the shortening in a skillet, then add the crumbs and brown. Add the salt, celery salt, pepper and onion. Cook the cabbage for 5 minutes in boiling salted water and drain. Alternate layers of tomatoes, cabbage and crumb mixture in a greased 1 1/2-quart casserole with the crumb mixture on top. Sprinkle the cheese over the crumb layer. Bake in 350-degree oven for 25 minutes. 6 servings.

Mrs. Melvin York, Camilla, Georgia

VEGETABLE-PARMESAN CASSEROLE

2 c. canned peas	1/2 c. chopped green pepper
2 c. canned green lima beans	1/2 c. sour cream
2 c. canned French-style	1/2 c. mayonnaise
green beans	1 c. grated Parmesan cheese

Drain the peas, lima beans and green beans and mix. Add remaining ingredients except cheese and mix well. Place in a 2-quart casserole and sprinkle with Parmesan cheese. Bake at 350 degrees for 45 minutes. 8 servings.

Mrs. Carl Kidd, Maryville, Tennessee

CORN-TOMATO CASSEROLE

2 c. cut fresh corn	2 tsp. salt
1 1/2 c. diced fresh tomatoes	1/4 tsp. pepper
1/4 c. chopped onions	1 tbsp. melted butter or
1/4 c. sliced celery	margarine
1 1/2 c. toasted bread cubes	3 eggs, well beaten

Combine all ingredients and turn into a greased 1-quart casserole. Cover the casserole and place in a pan of hot water. Bake at 325 degrees for 1 hour and 30 minutes or until knife inserted in center comes out clean. Garnish with paprika. 6 servings.

Mrs. Nadine Crews, Summertown, Tennessee

MEATLESS TAMALE CASSEROLE

2 c. cornmeal	1 No. 2 can cream-style corn
3 c. milk	1 No. 2 can tomatoes, sieved
3 eggs, beaten	2 tsp. chili powder
1 tsp. salt	2 cloves of garlic, minced
1 can ripe pitted olives, chopped	2 med. onions, chopped fine

Combine first 5 ingredients in a double boiler and cook for 15 minutes. Mix remaining ingredients and mix with cornmeal mixture. Turn into a baking dish. Bake at 400 degrees for 45 minutes to 1 hour. 8 servings.

Mrs. Ivan Block, Hereford, Texas

CAULIFLOWER AND TOMATOES AU GRATIN

1 lge. cauliflower	1 c. grated Cheddar cheese
4 med. tomatoes	3 c. medium cream sauce

Separate the cauliflower into flowerets. Peel and slice the tomatoes. Cook the cauliflower in salted water until tender, then drain and place in a baking dish. Arrange tomato slices around and on top of the cauliflower. Melt half the cheese in the cream sauce and pour over the cauliflower and tomatoes. Cover with remaining cheese. Bake at 400 degrees for 20 minutes or until brown. 8 servings.

Mrs. Effie Gaynon, Chamblee, Georgia

VEGETABLE SALAD

1 c. finely cut cabbage	Salt and pepper to taste
1 c. cold boiled beets	1 head lettuce
1 c. cold boiled carrots	1/2 c. pimento strips
1 c. cold boiled potatoes	1 c. French dressing
1 c. finely cut celery	

Soak the cabbage in cold water for 1 hour, then drain and add the beets, carrots, potatoes and celery. Add salt and pepper and mix well. Place servings on lettuce leaves. Top with strips of pimento and serve with French dressing. One teaspoon onion juice may be added to dressing.

Mrs. Clarence Broughton, Harrodsburg, Kentucky

Herbed Creamed Onions and Peas (below)

HERBED CREAMED ONIONS AND PEAS

1 lb. small white onions	**2 tbsp. flour**
1 1/2 tsp. salt	**1 c. milk**
1 lb. fresh peas, shelled	**1/4 tsp. ground basil**
2 tbsp. butter or margarine	**1/8 tsp. pepper**

Pour enough boiling water over onions to cover. Let stand for 5 minutes, then peel. Place in a saucepan with 1 teaspoon salt and 1 inch boiling water and bring to boiling point. Boil, uncovered, for 5 minutes. Cover and cook for 15 minutes or until tender. Drain. Cook the peas in another saucepan in boiling, salted water for 5 minutes or until done, then drain. Melt the butter in a saucepan and blend in flour. Remove from heat and stir in the milk. Cook over medium heat, stirring, until thickened. Stir in remaining salt, basil and pepper. Place the peas in a serving bowl and place onions in center of peas. Pour the sauce over onions. 4 servings.

BAKED EGGPLANT PALERMO

2 lge. eggplant	**1 tsp. sweet basil**
2 4-oz. cans mushrooms	**2 tbsp. instant minced onion**
2 sm. green peppers, chopped	**2 sm. tomatoes, chopped**
1/2 c. butter	**2 sm. cans artichoke hearts,**
1 tsp. garlic powder	**drained**
1 tsp. salt	**1 c. Parmesan cheese**
1 1/2 tsp. oregano	

Cut the eggplant in half lengthwise. Scoop out the pulp, leaving 1/2-inch thick shell. Dice the pulp and reserve. Boil the shells in salted water until tender and drain. Place cut side up in a baking dish. Saute the mushrooms, peppers and eggplant pulp in butter, then add remaining ingredients except cheese. Simmer for 3 to 4 minutes, then stir in 3/4 cup cheese. Spoon lightly into eggplant shells and sprinkle with remaining cheese. Bake in 350-degree oven for 20 minutes or until cheese is brown. 4 servings.

Mrs. Joe H. Nichols, Dumas, Arkansas

VEGETABLE DISH

2 or 3 tbsp. flour
1/2 stick butter or margarine
1 1/2 c. milk
1/2 lb. cheese, grated

2 cans sm. whole potatoes
2 cans sm. onions
2 cans English peas

Brown the flour in butter, then add the milk. Cook, stirring constantly, until thickened. Add the cheese and cook, stirring, until cheese melts. Place the potatoes and onions in a casserole and add the peas. Pour the cheese sauce over the vegetables. Bake at 350 degrees for 30 minutes or until brown.

Mrs. B. G. Greenway, Colbert, Oklahoma

TABOULI

1/2 lb. bulgur or cracked
    wheat
4 fresh tomatoes, cut in cubes
1 clove of garlic,
    minced (opt.)
1 sm. bunch scallions,
    coarsely chopped

6 parsley sprigs, finely
    chopped
4 mint leaves, chopped
Olive oil
1/4 c. lemon juice
1/2 tsp. salt
Lettuce leaves

Soak the bulgur in water for 15 minutes, then drain thoroughly. Combine the tomatoes, garlic, scallions, parsley, mint, 3 tablespoons olive oil, lemon juice and salt and mix. Add the bulgur and toss lightly. Arrange on lettuce leaves on individual salad plates and sprinkle olive oil over each serving. 8 servings.

Mrs. Annie R. Gonzales, Baton Rouge, Louisiana

ASHEVILLE SALAD

2 3-oz. packages cream
    cheese
2 cans tomato soup
2 tbsp. unflavored gelatin
1/3 c. cold water

1/3 c. minced celery
1/3 c. minced green pepper
1 c. minced onion
1/2 c. chopped pecans
1 c. mayonnaise

Combine the cream cheese and soup in a saucepan and heat over low heat until mixed. Soften the gelatin in the cold water. Add to soup mixture and stir until dissolved. Cool. Add vegetables, pecans and mayonnaise and pour into a mold. Chill until firm. Serve on lettuce leaves with additional mayonnaise.

Mrs. E. L. Wolf, Atlanta, Georgia

SALADE NICOISE

5 tomatoes, quartered	1 family-sized can chunk
1/2 onion, sliced	tuna, drained
1 green pepper, sliced	8 anchovy fillets
1/4 c. sliced radishes	2 hard-cooked eggs, quartered
4 stalks celery, chopped	10 ripe pitted olives
1 clove of garlic, crushed	

Chill all ingredients well. Place in a large salad bowl in order listed.

Dressing

2 tbsp. wine vinegar	Pinch of basil
6 tbsp. oil	

Combine all ingredients in jar and cover. Shake well. Pour over salad.

Mrs. Dennis Smith, Houston, Texas

BEANS AND PEAS MELANGE

1 can green beans	1 tbsp. (heaping) butter
1 can black-eyed peas	Dash of pepper
2 strips smoked bacon	Parsley

Combine the beans and peas in a saucepan. Fry the bacon until crisp and break into small pieces. Add to the bean mixture and simmer for 30 minutes or until most of the liquid has been absorbed. Add the butter, pepper and a small amount of parsley.

Mrs. George Johns, Orlando, Florida

SAUCY SOUTHERN CASSEROLE

1/3 c. canned milk	1/4 c. sliced celery
3/4 c. mayonnaise	1/4 c. diced green pepper
1/2 tsp. salt	1 No. 2 can whole tomatoes
1/8 tsp. pepper	3 c. cooked asparagus spears
1 tsp. fresh lemon juice	2 tbsp. margarine
1/4 c. fresh orange juice	1 pkg. onion rings
2 tbsp. cooking oil	

Combine the milk and mayonnaise and heat for 5 minutes in the top of a double boiler. Add salt, pepper, lemon juice and orange juice, stirring constantly. Pour the oil into a heavy skillet. Add the celery and green pepper and brown lightly. Drain the tomatoes and add to the celery mixture. Place the asparagus in a buttered casserole. Add the tomato mixture and cover with the sauce. Top with the onion rings. Bake for 30 minutes in a 350-degree oven. Serve hot.

Mrs. John Roberts, Lineville, Alabama

DINNER TIME-SAVER

2 c. diced potatoes	**2 tsp. salt**
2 c. chopped celery	**1/4 tsp. pepper**
2 c. hamburger	**1 tsp. vinegar (opt.)**
1 c. sliced onions	**1/2 c. butter or margarine**
2 c. canned tomatoes	**Crushed crackers (opt.)**

Alternate layers of the potatoes, celery, hamburger, onions and tomatoes in a greased casserole, sprinkling each layer with salt, pepper and vinegar and dotting with butter. Top with a thin layer of cracker crumbs. Bake at 350 degrees for 1 hour and 45 minutes. 6-8 servings.

Mary Porter, Knoxville, Tennessee

GARDEN SKILLET SUPPER

2 zucchini	**1/2 c. flour**
1 med. eggplant, peeled	**2 green peppers, cut in strips**
1/2 c. butter	**2 tomatoes, cut in wedges**
1 c. thinly sliced onions	**1 tsp. salt**
1 clove of garlic, finely	**1/4 tsp. oregano**
chopped	**1/8 tsp. pepper**

Cut the zucchini and eggplant in 1/2-inch slices. Melt the butter in an electric frypan or large skillet. Saute the onions and garlic in butter until onions are tender. Dip zucchini and eggplant in flour to lightly coat. Add to onion mixture along with green peppers and cover. Simmer for 30 minutes. Add the tomatoes, salt, oregano and pepper and cook for 15 minutes longer. 8-10 servings.

Garden Skillet Supper (above)

159

INDIAN FARE

1 1/2 lb. ground beef
1 lge. onion, chopped
1 No. 2 can whole tomatoes

1 No. 2 can golden hominy
Salt and pepper to taste
1 1/2 c. grated cheese

Brown the ground beef and onion in a small amount of fat, then add the tomatoes and hominy. Season to taste. Bake at 350 degrees for about 45 minutes. Sprinkle with the cheese and bake for 15 minutes longer. Serve immediately. 8 servings.

Nancy M. Riley, Macon, Georgia

PEAS AND CORN IN SOUR CREAM

3 c. canned peas
1 sm. onion, chopped
1 stalk celery, chopped
1 tsp. parsley, chopped
2 tbsp. margarine

2 c. whole kernel corn
1/2 tsp. savory
Salt and pepper to taste
1/2 c. sour cream
1 tsp. lemon juice

Bring the peas to a boil and cook for 5 minutes. Cook the onion, celery and parsley in margarine for 5 minutes, then add the peas, corn, savory, salt and pepper. Add the sour cream and lemon juice and serve immediately. 6 servings.

Mrs. G. K. Clyme, Reidsville, North Carolina

TIELA

1/2 c. grated Parmesan cheese
1/2 c. bread crumbs
2 tbsp. chopped parsley
1/4 tsp. salt
1/4 tsp. garlic salt

1/4 tsp. oregano
3 med. zucchini, sliced
4 med. potatoes, peeled and sliced
1 lge. can tomatoes
2 tbsp. salad or olive oil

Combine the cheese, bread crumbs, parsley and seasonings. Place a layer of zucchini and potatoes in a baking dish. Sprinkle generously with the cheese mixture, then add a layer of tomatoes. Repeat until all ingredients are used. Pour the oil evenly over the top layer. Cover dish with foil. Bake in 350-degree oven until zucchini and potatoes are tender. Remove the foil about 15 minutes before taking from oven to allow top to brown.

Mrs. Brenda Jo McNabb, Clarksburg, West Virginia

PEAS AND POTATOES SUPREME

1 1-lb. can peas
5 med. potatoes, boiled
3 tbsp. margarine, melted

1/2 tsp. Worcestershire sauce
1/2 tsp. salt
1/2 tsp. pepper

Bring the peas to a boil and pour into a casserole. Arrange the potatoes around the peas. Mix the margarine, Worcestershire sauce, salt and pepper and pour over the potatoes. Bake in 350-degree oven until heated through.

Mrs. Nancy Carter, Fayetteville, Arkansas

VEGETABLE CRISPS

1 c. fine dry bread crumbs	2 slightly beaten eggs
1/4 c. grated Parmesan cheese	1 c. fresh cauliflowerets
1 tsp. paprika	1 c. crosswise-sliced carrots
1 tsp. salt	Salad oil

Combine the bread crumbs, cheese, paprika and 1/2 teaspoon salt in a bowl. Combine the eggs, 1 tablespoon water and remaining salt in another bowl. Dip the vegetables in the egg mixture, then in crumb mixture. Repeat dipping. Pour enough salad oil into a fondue pot to fill to depth of 2 inches and heat to 375 degrees. Place fondue pot over fondue burner. Spear vegetables with fondue forks. Fry in hot oil for 2 to 3 minutes. 6-8 servings.

Mrs. Ira Barry, Burnsville, North Carolina

CALICO CASSEROLE

3 slices bacon	2 c. fresh or frozen corn
1/4 c. chopped onion	1/2 tsp. salt
2 tbsp. flour	1/8 tsp. pepper
2 c. chopped tomatoes	1 tsp. sugar
1/4 c. diced green pepper	

Fry the bacon until crisp. Remove from pan and crumble or break into small pieces. Pour off all but 2 tablespoons fat, then add the onion and brown lightly. Blend in the flour and add tomatoes, green pepper and corn. Blend in the salt, pepper and sugar. Pour the vegetable mixture into a buttered casserole. Bake for 15 minutes at 400 degrees. Sprinkle bacon on top. 6 servings.

Mrs. George Harrison, Huntington, West Virginia

VEGETABLE PIE

4 cooked potatoes	1 c. white sauce
3 hard-boiled eggs	Finely grated cheese
3 tomatoes	1 sm. onion, minced

Slice the potatoes, eggs and tomatoes. Place a layer of potatoes in a shallow baking dish and add a layer of eggs. Add another layer of potatoes, then tomatoes. Top with potatoes and pour the sauce over all. Sprinkle with cheese and onion. Bake in 350-degree oven for 20 to 30 minutes.

Mrs. Bill Williamson, Cleveland, Tennessee

Green Peas and Zucchini Salad (below)

GREEN PEAS AND ZUCCHINI SALAD

1 lb. small zucchini, thinly sliced	1 env. Italian salad dressing mix
1 10-oz. package frozen green peas and pearl onions	2 tbsp. wine or cider vinegar
	Crisp salad greens

Cook the zucchini in 2 cups boiling, salted water for 1 minute, then drain. Cook peas and onions according to package directions. Prepare the salad dressing mix according to package directions. Combine the vegetables with 1/2 cup salad dressing and vinegar and cover. Chill for at least 4 hours, stirring gently once or twice. Line a chilled bowl with salad greens and spoon in the marinated vegetables. Serve with remaining salad dressing, if desired. 7-8 servings.

GREEN BROCCOLI RING AND BEETS

2 pkg. frozen broccoli	3 eggs, beaten
2 tbsp. butter	3/4 c. mayonnaise
3 tbsp. flour	1 sm. can beets
1 can evaporated milk	1 tbsp. vinegar
1/2 tsp. salt	

Cook the broccoli according to package directions, then drain and mash. Melt the butter in a saucepan, then stir in the flour. Add the milk gradually, stirring constantly and cook until thickened. Add the salt. Stir in the eggs, gradually, and add the mayonnaise and broccoli. Place in an oiled ring mold and set in a pan of hot water. Bake at 350 degrees for 45 minutes. Unmold. Heat the beets and vinegar together and spoon in the center of the broccoli ring. 8 servings.

Jimmie Garvin Harris, Aiken, South Carolina

TOMATO-OKRA PILAU

3 slices bacon	Salt and pepper to taste
1 sm. onion, chopped	2 c. rice
2 c. stewed tomatoes	1 tsp. salt
2 c. sliced okra	2 qt. water

Fry the bacon till crisp and crumble. Brown the onion in the bacon drippings, then add the tomatoes and okra. Simmer until done, stirring occasionally and add salt and pepper. Cook the rice in salted water for 12 minutes and drain. Fold into the tomato mixture and place in the top of a double boiler. Let steam for 15 minutes, then serve topped with bacon. 6-8 servings.

Rosanne Looney, Texarkana, Texas

VEGETABLE-SALMON CASSEROLE WITH CHEESE PINWHEELS

1 10-oz. package frozen mixed vegetables	1/4 tsp. salt
	1/4 tsp. curry powder
1 1-lb. can salmon, drained	1/4 tsp. ground pepper
1 can cream of mushroom soup	2 c. prepared biscuit mix
Milk	1/2 c. shredded Cheddar cheese

Cook the frozen mixed vegetables according to package directions and drain. Mix the salmon, vegetables, soup, 1/4 cup milk and seasonings. Turn into a 6 x 12 x 2-inch baking dish. Combine the biscuit mix and 2/3 cup milk according to package directions. Roll out 1/8-inch thick. Sprinkle with the shredded cheese. Roll up as for jelly roll. Cut in 1-inch pieces. Arrange over the salmon mixture. Bake in 375-degree oven for 30 minutes or until the biscuits are golden brown. 6 servings.

Mrs. Rosie Gibson, Earle, Arkansas

CORN AND EGGPLANT BAKE

2 c. peeled cubed eggplant	1 tsp. salt
1/2 c. drained whole kernel corn	1 3-oz. package cream cheese
3 tbsp. minced green pepper	2 eggs, well beaten
3 tbsp. minced green onion	1 c. cottage cheese
1 c. tomato juice	1/2 c. soft bread crumbs

Boil the eggplant in salted water until tender and drain thoroughly in a colander. Add the corn, green pepper and onion. Heat the tomato juice and salt in a double boiler. Break the cream cheese in small pieces and add to the hot juice, stirring until blended. Pour the tomato mixture gradually into the eggs, stirring constantly, then blend in the cottage cheese. Add the eggplant mixture and bread crumbs and place in a buttered 1 1/2-quart casserole. Bake at 350 degrees for 45 minutes or until firm. 6 servings.

Ann Elsie Schmetzer, Madisonville, Kentucky

BROCCOLI PIE

4 c. chopped broccoli	3 tbsp. mayonnaise
1 pkg. frozen lima beans	1 tsp. prepared mustard
1 c. cooked carrot slices	3 hard-boiled eggs
3 c. milk	Crushed cornflakes
2 tbsp. minced onion	Butter

Cook all the vegetables in salted water until tender, but not completely done. Combine the milk, onion, mayonnaise and prepared mustard. Slice the eggs and arrange the vegetables and eggs in layers, beginning with broccoli, and spoon the milk sauce over each layer. Cover with the sauce and sprinkle with crushed cornflakes. Dot with butter. Bake at 325 degrees for 25 minutes. 8-10 servings.

Mrs. Dorothy Butler, Orangeburg, South Carolina

COLCANNON

4 lge. carrots	1 med. onion, halved
1 sm. parsnip, chopped (opt.)	Salt and pepper to taste
1 sm. cabbage, chopped	1 pt. cream
1/4 med. turnip, chopped	1/4 lb. butter
15 lge. potatoes, halved	

Scrape and chop the carrots and place in a saucepan with 1 cup water. Add the parsnip and cook for 10 minutes, then add the cabbage and turnip. Cook until almost done and add the potatoes and onion. Cook until done and drain. Mash the vegetables with a potato masher and add salt and pepper. Heat the cream and add with the butter to the vegetables and mix well. 8 servings.

Mrs. Jennie Stewart, Dallas, Texas

SAVORY JULIENNE VEGETABLES

2 lge. yellow onions	2 tbsp. salad oil
2 c. celery	2 tbsp. cold water
2 tbsp. soy sauce	

Cut the onions into thin slices lengthwise and the celery into thin diagonal slices. Combine all ingredients, then cover and steam for 3 to 5 minutes, stirring once or twice. Do not overcook. Cooked julienne slices of meat may be added. 4 servings.

Mrs. Maenell James, Ft. Walton, Florida

VEGETABLE PUFFS

3 or 4 eggs, beaten	1 tsp. salt
3 c. mixed vegetables	Dash of pepper
2 to 3 c. oats	2 tbsp. fat
1 tbsp. chopped onion	

Combine all the ingredients except fat and mix well. Drop by spoonfuls into hot fat in a skillet and brown on both sides. 6 servings.

Mrs. Marjorie Murrell, Tulsa, Oklahoma

SWEET AND SOUR CARROTS AND ONIONS

8 sm. carrots, cooked	1/4 tsp. salt
4 to 8 sm. onions, cooked	2 tbsp. sugar
2 tbsp. butter or margarine	2 tbsp. vinegar
2 tbsp. flour	1/4 tsp. paprika

Drain the carrots and onions, reserving the carrot liquid and add water to measure 1 cup. Melt the butter, then add the flour, salt, sugar, vinegar, paprika and carrot stock. Cook until thickened, stirring constantly. Add the vegetables and cook over low heat for 15 to 20 minutes, stirring occasionally. 4 servings.

Mrs. Sally Hughes, Blytheville, Arkansas

SCALLOPED BROCCOLI AND ONIONS IMPERIAL

1 10-oz. package frozen broccoli	1/3 c. milk
1 1-lb. can sm. whole white onions	1/2 to 1 tsp. curry powder
1 can cream of mushroom soup	1/4 c. toasted slivered almonds

Cook the broccoli according to package directions, then drain. Drain the onions. Arrange the broccoli in spoke fashion in a 1 1/2-quart shallow, round casserole and place onions between broccoli. Stir soup until smooth. Blend in the milk and curry and pour over vegetables. Top with almonds. Bake at 350 degrees for 30 minutes. 4 servings.

Scalloped Broccoli and Onions Imperial (above)

Vegetable Medley Casserole (below)

VEGETABLE MEDLEY CASSEROLE

2 c. cut green beans
2 c. celery crescents or
   slices
2 c. coarsely shredded cabbage
1/4 c. butter
1/4 c. flour

2 c. milk
1 c. shredded Cheddar cheese
Salt and pepper to taste
2 peeled tomatoes, thickly
   sliced

Cook the beans in boiling, salted water until almost tender. Add the celery and cabbage and cook for 2 to 3 minutes or until celery is heated through but still crisp. Drain thoroughly. Melt the butter in a saucepan over low heat and blend in flour. Add the milk and cook, stirring constantly, until smooth and thickened. Add the cheese and stir over low heat until melted. Season with salt and pepper and fold in cooked vegetables gently. Place in a buttered, shallow baking dish and top with tomato slices. Season the tomato slices with salt and pepper and sprinkle with additional cheese. Bake in a 400-degree oven for 12 to 15 minutes or until heated and lightly browned. Serve at once. May be broiled until browned instead of baked, if desired. 6 servings.

SMORGASBORD CASSEROLE

1 15-oz. can cut green beans,
   drained
1 15-oz. can cut asparagus
   spears, drained
1 c. chopped cooked ham
2 tbsp. butter, melted

1/4 c. flour
2 c. milk
3/4 tsp. salt
1/8 tsp. celery seed
1 1/2 tbsp. mustard
2 hard-cooked eggs, chopped

Arrange the beans, asparagus and ham in layers in a greased 2-quart casserole. Blend the butter and flour and stir in the milk. Cook, stirring constantly, until thick and smooth, then add the salt, celery seed and mustard. Pour over the vegetables and ham and top with the eggs. Bake at 350 degrees for 25 minutes. 6 servings.

Mrs. Jinnie Mueller, Vicksburg, Mississippi

INDIAN SUMMER SUCCOTASH

1 qt. fresh butter beans	3 tomatoes, peeled
1 slice bacon	2 stalks celery, chopped
1 tbsp. butter	Salt and pepper to taste
3 potatoes, cut up	1 c. fresh corn
1 sm. onion	

Pour 1 quart water in a saucepan and bring to a boil. Add the butter beans, bacon and butter and cook for 30 minutes. Add the potatoes, onion, tomatoes, celery, salt and pepper and cook over low heat for 1 hour. Add the corn ten minutes before serving time and reheat. 6 servings.

Mrs. J. W. Bonniville, Suffolk, Virginia

SPINACH AND CORN PARMESAN

1 10-oz. package frozen spinach	1/4 tsp. pepper
1 tbsp. dried onion	1/4 c. fine bread crumbs
1 can cream-style corn	2 tbsp. grated Parmesan cheese
1 tsp. vinegar	2 tbsp. melted butter or margarine
1/2 tsp. salt	

Thaw the spinach at room temperature and drain. Combine the spinach, onion, corn, vinegar, salt and pepper in a lightly greased baking dish. Blend the crumbs, cheese and melted butter and sprinkle over the vegetables. Bake at 400 degrees for 20 minutes.

Mrs. David Hill, Virginia Beach, Virginia

VEGETABLE-PEANUT DISH

2 med. sweet potatoes	1 can mushroom sauce or soup
1/4 c. margarine	1 c. milk
1/2 c. brown sugar	1 beaten egg
1/2 c. sliced carrots	1 c. chopped peanuts
1/3 c. chopped celery (opt.)	1 c. grated cheese
1 c. drained English peas	6 to 8 slices luncheon meat

Peel and slice the sweet potatoes, then line a baking dish with the slices, margarine and brown sugar. Add the carrots, celery, peas and sauce. Combine the milk and egg and pour over the mixture. Top with the peanuts, cheese and luncheon meat. Bake in 350-degree oven for 1 hour.

Mrs. Fred Disher, Winston-Salem, North Carolina

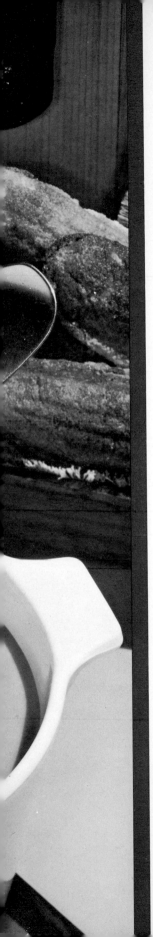

vegetable soups

Homemade soup — what other dish says so much about the care you take in preparing your family's food! Of the many soups which simmer for hours on the back burner of your stove, among the most popular family-pleasers are vegetable soups.

Hot or cold, thick or thin, vegetable soups are versatile dishes which can play an important role on every occasion. In the heat of a summer's evening, get your meal off to a pleasing start with Frosty Cucumber Soup. It has a light touch certain to be welcomed at the end of a long, warm day. And it is the just-right preface to whatever main dish you may be featuring.

Many soups created by southern homemakers are a meal in themselves. Vegetable Beef Soup, for example, is the perfect lunch or supper dish — try it with crusty chunks of fresh bread and fruit dessert. Another popular and hearty soup is Minestrone. Originally an Italian vegetable soup, southern women have revised the recipe to suit their families' tastes — and the recipe you'll find in the pages that follow is certain to bring compliments from your family, too.

Even pea soup has a southern accent in these pages — Dilled Split Pea Soup is a thick, rich dish you'll serve again and again. In fact, every one of these home-tested recipes can be depended upon for flavorful results — every time!

169

REFRESHING CATALONIA VEGETABLE SOUP

1 c. chopped peeled tomatoes	1 sm. clove of garlic, minced
1/2 c. finely chopped green pepper	2 1/2 tbsp. wine vinegar
1/2 c. finely chopped celery	2 tbsp. olive oil
1/2 c. finely chopped peeled cucumber	1 tsp. salt
1/4 c. finely chopped onion	1/4 tsp. pepper
2 tsp. finely chopped parsley	1/2 tsp. Worcestershire sauce
2 tsp. chopped chives	2 c. tomato juice

Combine all the ingredients in a bowl and mix well. Cover and chill for several hours. Serve in chilled cups. 6 servings.

Mrs. Joan Shannon, El Paso, Texas

WHITE BEAN SOUP

2 c. navy beans	1 celery stalk, chopped
1 hambone with meat	1 clove of garlic, minced
1/2 c. cooked mashed potatoes	1/4 c. finely chopped parsley
3 onions, finely chopped	

Place the beans and 3 quarts water in a kettle and soak overnight. Add the hambone and enough water to cover and bring to a boil. Reduce heat and simmer for 1 hour. Add the potatoes and stir until well mixed. Remove hambone and cool. Remove meat from bone and chop. Add to soup. Add the onions, celery, garlic and parsley. Simmer for 1 hour.

Mrs. Lillian Herman, Midwest City, Oklahoma

RAIL-SPLITTER SOUP

8 slices bacon	1 1/4 c. packaged precooked rice
1 c. diced ham	1 to 2 tsp. salt
1 1/2 c. mixed vegetables	1/8 tsp. pepper
3 1/2 c. canned tomatoes	1 tbsp. parsley flakes
3 c. water	

Fry the bacon in a skillet until crisp. Drain and crumble. Pour 2 tablespoons drippings from skillet into a kettle. Add the ham and cook until lightly browned. Add the bacon and remaining ingredients except parsley and bring to a boil. Reduce heat and simmer until rice is cooked and vegetables are tender, adding water, if needed. Add parsley just before serving. 6-8 servings.

Mrs. Betty DeVoe, Nashville, Tennessee

FROSTY CUCUMBER SOUP

1 med. cucumber	2 cans frozen cream of potato soup, thawed
1 c. milk	

1/2 tsp. salt	1 c. heavy cream
1/8 tsp. pepper	Chopped chives

Peel the cucumber and remove the seeds. Dice and place in a blender container with the milk. Blend until the cucumber is finely minced. Add 1 can soup and blend. Pour half the mixture into a bowl. Blend the second can of soup with the remaining mixture in the blender. Combine in the bowl with remaining ingredients except chives. Chill for several hours. Spoon into cups and sprinkle with chopped chives. 6 servings.

Mrs. Eleanor Maddox, Meridian, Mississippi

VEGETABLE-RICE SOUP

1 lb. lean beef, cut into sm. pieces	1/4 green pepper, cut fine
1 carrot, sliced thin	1 potato, cut up
1 stalk celery, cut fine	1 c. fresh or frozen corn
1 sm. onion, cut fine	1 qt. cooked tomatoes
1 c. green lima beans	1/2 c. cooked rice
1 c. chopped cabbage	1/2 c. tomato catsup
	Salt and pepper to taste

Combine the beef, carrot, celery, onion, lima beans, cabbage and green pepper in a large kettle and add 2 cups water. Bring to a boil and cook until the beef is tender. Add the potato and corn and cook until tender. Add remaining ingredients and cook until all ingredients are done.

Mrs. Robert Seals, Dallas, Georgia

FAMILY-STYLE LENTIL SOUP

1/2 c. bacon drippings	8 c. beef broth or bouillon
1/2 lb. onions, thinly sliced	1 tbsp. sugar
3 lge. carrots, chopped	2 tsp. pepper
2 c. finely chopped celery	1/2 tsp. garlic powder
1/3 c. flour	2 bay leaves
3 1/4 lb. lentils, washed	6 frankfurters, diagonally sliced
2 meaty hambones	Salt to taste

Combine the bacon drippings, onions, carrots and celery in a 4-gallon kettle. Cook, covered, for 20 minutes. Stir in the flour, then add remaining ingredients except the frankfurters and salt. Simmer, uncovered, for 1 hour. Cut meat from bones and chop. Return the meat and bones to the kettle and simmer for 2 hours. Remove the bones before serving and add the sliced frankfurters and salt.

Mrs. Andrew Davis, Dothan, Alabama

171

Swiss Potato Soup (below)

SWISS POTATO SOUP

2 tbsp. butter	1/2 tsp. salt
1/4 c. chopped onion	Dash of pepper
2 c. seasoned mashed potatoes	Crisp bacon pieces
2 c. milk	Chopped chives
2 c. shredded Swiss cheese	

Melt the butter in a saucepan. Add the onion and saute until transparent. Add the potatoes. Add the milk and stir to blend well. Blend in the cheese, salt and pepper and place over low heat until heated through, stirring until cheese melts. Do not boil. Garnish with bacon and chives. 5 1/2 cups.

CREAMED VEGETABLE SOUP

1 c. diced carrots	1/2 lb. salt pork
1 c. cubed potatoes	1/2 c. flour
1 bell pepper, diced	1 qt. milk
1 c. diced celery	Salt to taste
1/2 c. sliced green onions	

Cook the carrots, potatoes, bell pepper, celery and green onions in boiling, salted water until tender, then drain. Wash the salt pork and cut into cubes. Cook in a large saucepan over low heat until brown, stirring frequently. Add the flour and mix well. Stir in the milk and cook, stirring constantly, until thickened. Season with salt. Add the vegetables and heat through.

Photograph for this recipe on page 5.

GARDEN VEGETABLE STEW

2 qt. beef stock	Salt and pepper to taste
2 onions, chopped	4 peeled tomatoes, cut in
4 carrots, cubed	wedges
1 c. chopped celery	4 potatoes, cubed
1 bell pepper, chopped	2 c. whole kernel corn
1 hot pepper	1 c. cut green beans (opt.)
1/2 tsp. thyme	1/2 c. sliced okra (opt.)
1/2 tsp. oregano	

Pour the stock into a kettle and bring to a boil. Add the onions, carrots, celery, bell pepper, hot pepper, thyme, oregano, salt and pepper and simmer until carrots are tender. Add remaining ingredients and simmer until vegetables are done, adding water, if needed. Remove the hot pepper. Thicken with cornstarch mixed with water, if desired.

Photograph for this recipe on cover.

DOUKHABOR BORSCHT

3 med. potatoes	1 sm. cabbage, shredded
1 bunch carrots	1 1-lb. 12-oz. can tomatoes
2 lge. onions, diced	1 tbsp. chopped dill
1/2 c. butter	1/2 pt. sour cream

Peel the potatoes and carrots and dice. Cook in 3 quarts boiling, salted water in a large saucepan until tender. Fry the onions in butter until golden brown. Add cabbage and fry until wilted, stirring frequently. Add the tomatoes and dill and simmer for several minutes. Add to the potato mixture and bring to a boil. Reduce heat and simmer for 30 to 45 minutes. Stir in the sour cream and heat through. Three quarts beef broth may be substituted for boiling, salted water. 6-8 servings.

Mrs. Jennifer Lacey, Valdosta, Georgia

HOT CREME VICHYSSOISE

4 green onions, chopped	4 chicken bouillon cubes
1 med. onion, chopped	4 c. light cream
6 tbsp. butter	Salt and pepper to taste
4 med. potatoes, quartered	1 pt. sour cream
1 qt. water	

Cook onions in butter in a kettle over low heat until tender. Add the potatoes, water and bouillon cubes and cook for 30 minutes. Mash the potatoes. Add the cream, salt and pepper and bring to a boil. Remove from heat. Add the sour cream. 6 servings.

Mrs. Thomas Smith, Baton Rouge, Louisiana

MINESTRONE

1 meaty beef or veal soupbone	3 carrots, grated
Cooking oil	1 leek or onion, minced
10 c. water	1 med. turnip, grated
Dash of Worcestershire sauce	1 c. string beans, cut into strips
Salt and pepper to taste	1 c. broken spaghetti
Garlic salt to taste	1/4 c. butter
2 med. potatoes, grated	Grated Gruyere cheese

Brown the soupbone in a small amount of oil in a kettle, then cover with the water. Add seasonings and cook until the meat is tender. Remove meat from bone and place back in kettle. Add vegetables and cook over low heat for 1 hour and 30 minutes, adding water, if needed. Add the spaghetti and cook for 9 to 12 minutes. Add the butter. Ladle into soup bowls and sprinkle with cheese. 8 servings.

Mrs. Donald S. Cramen, Little Creek Amphib Base, Virginia

VEGETABLE-BEEF SOUP

2 tbsp. butter or margarine	1 c. lima beans
1 lb. ground beef	1 c. green peas
1 c. chopped onions	2 1-lb. cans tomatoes
1 c. sliced carrots	1 can sliced okra, drained
1 c. sliced celery	4 c. water
1/2 c. rice	1/2 tsp. basil
1 c. macaroni	1/4 tsp. thyme
Salt to taste	1 bay leaf

Combine the butter, ground beef and onions in a large kettle. Cook over medium heat till browned, stirring with a fork to break up the ground beef. Add the remaining ingredients and mix well. Bring to a boil, then reduce heat. Simmer, covered, for 1 hour or until the vegetables are tender.

Mrs. Clarence Hall, Sylvia, North Carolina

NORMANDY SOUP POT

6 lge. potatoes	1/2 c. sliced celery and leaves
3 med. leeks	3 sprigs of parsley
2 med. carrots	2 tbsp. butter or margarine
4 10-oz. packages frozen	2 tbsp. salt
Brussels sprouts	1 tsp. monosodium glutamate
3 qt. boiling water	1/4 tsp. pepper

Peel and quarter the potatoes. Cut the leeks in 2-inch lengths. Scrape and quarter the carrots. Place the potatoes, leeks, carrots and Brussels sprouts in boiling water in a kettle and cover. Simmer for 30 minutes. Stir in the celery, parsley, butter and seasonings and simmer for 1 hour longer. 10 servings.

Mrs. James Potter, Winston-Salem, North Carolina

OVERNIGHT LENTIL SOUP

1 ham hock
1 c. dried lentils
1 carrot, finely diced

1 med. onion, finely diced
Salt and pepper to taste

Place the ham hock in a kettle in enough water to cover. Cook until very tender. Remove ham hock and cool. Remove ham from bone and place in the kettle. Add the lentils and soak overnight. Add the carrot and onion and cook until lentils are tender. Season with salt and pepper. 4-6 servings.

Justine C. Irwin, Norman, Oklahoma

QUICK KIDNEY BEAN SOUP

1 1-lb. can kidney beans
1 1-lb. can tomatoes
2 med. onions, minced
1/2 c. diced celery
1/2 c. water
1 tsp. salt

1 tsp. sugar
2 tsp. angostura aromatic
   bitters
Lemon or hard-cooked egg
   slices (opt.)

Combine the kidney beans with tomatoes, onions, celery, water, salt and sugar in a saucepan and heat to boiling point. Reduce heat and simmer until beans are very tender. Add the angostura bitters and beat with a wooden spoon or whisk until beans are broken into small pieces. Add more salt, if needed. Garnish with slices of lemon. 6 servings.

Quick Kidney Bean Soup (above)

VEGETABLE-BARLEY SOUP

1 hambone with meat	2 1/4 c. tomatoes
6 c. water	2 med. green peppers, chopped
2 med. onions, sliced	1 med. potato, diced
1 clove of garlic, minced	2 med. carrots, diced
1 bay leaf	1/2 c. diced celery
Salt and pepper to taste	1/4 c. barley

Place the hambone, water, onions, garlic and bay leaf in a kettle and bring to a boil. Reduce heat and cover. Simmer for 1 hour. Remove hambone and cool. Remove meat from bone and chop. Return to the stock. Season stock with salt and pepper and add remaining ingredients. Cover and bring to a boil. Reduce heat. Simmer for 1 hour or until vegetables are tender.

Mrs. Lillian Herman, Bay City, Texas

JALAPENO VEGETABLE BEEF SOUP

1 soupbone with meat	1 No. 303 can tomatoes
4 c. water	1 tbsp. salt
1 med. onion, chopped	1/2 tsp. pepper
3 carrots, sliced	1/2 lb. Velveeta cheese
2 stalks celery, diced	1/4 c. jalapeno tomato sauce

Cook the soupbone in water in a kettle for 1 hour and 30 minutes. Add the onion, carrots and celery and cook for 30 minutes. Add tomatoes, salt and pepper and cook for 15 minutes. Melt the cheese in tomato sauce in a double boiler over medium heat. Add to soup and heat through. 6-8 servings.

Mrs. O. W. Norton, Fort Worth, Texas

GERMAN VEGETABLE SOUP

1 2-lb. ham or pork roast	2 c. diced potatoes
4 c. water	2 c. cut yellow string beans
1/2 c. chopped celery	1 c. diced carrots
1/4 c. chopped onion	1 c. peas

Place the ham in water in a kettle with celery and onion and simmer for 1 hour. Add the potatoes, beans, carrots and peas and simmer for 40 minutes longer. 4 servings.

Mrs. Mary Lou Zehnder, Shreveport, Louisiana

BEEF-NOODLE SOUP

2 lb. stew beef	4 potatoes, chopped
6 qt. water	1 med. onion, chopped
6 carrots, chopped	2 stalks celery, chopped

1 sm. cabbage, chopped	Salt and pepper
1 No. 2 can tomatoes, chopped	1 lb. medium noodles

Place the beef in a large saucepan and add water. Cook until beef is partially done. Add the vegetables and seasonings and cook for 1 hour and 30 minutes or until vegetables are done, adding water, if needed. Add the noodles and cook until tender, stirring frequently. 6-8 servings.

Erlene Paternostro, New Orleans, Louisiana

CABBAGE CHOWDER

4 c. shredded cabbage	1/2 tsp. sugar
2 c. sliced carrots	2 c. water
3 c. diced potatoes	2 tbsp. butter
1 tbsp. salt	4 c. milk
1/2 tsp. pepper	

Place all ingredients except butter and milk in a kettle and cook over low heat until vegetables are done. Add the butter and milk and heat through. 8 servings.

Mrs. Homer E. Miller, Flagstaff, Arizona

RUTABAGA SOUP

1 3-lb. beef shank bone with	4 qt. water
meat	2 lb. rutabagas, cubed
2 tbsp. salt	

Cook the shank bone in boiling, salted water until tender. Add the rutabagas and cook until rutabagas are tender, adding water, if needed. Remove the shank bone and cool. Remove meat from bone, then add to rutabagas. Mash rutabagas well. Bring soup to boiling point and serve. 6 servings.

Mrs. Edith L. Barker, Fairfax, South Carolina

GREEN BEAN-BUTTERMILK SOUP

3/4 lb. snapped green beans	1/2 tsp. pepper
1 qt. buttermilk	1 tbsp. flour

Cook the beans in boiling, salted water until done. Add the buttermilk and bring to a boil, stirring frequently. Add the pepper. Mix the flour and small amount of water and stir into the soup. Bring to a boil and remove from heat. Cool. Serve cold.

Mrs. H. H. Kierum, San Antonio, Texas

NAVY BEAN SOUP

1 c. dried navy beans	1 onion, sliced
1/2 c. chopped celery	3 tbsp. butter
1/2 tsp. salt	3 tbsp. flour
1/8 tsp. pepper	Juice of 1/2 lemon
1/4 tsp. dry mustard	

Place the beans in a kettle and cover with water. Soak for 8 hours, then drain. Add 5 cups water, celery and seasonings. Brown the onion in butter in a saucepan. Add the flour and stir until smooth. Add to beans and simmer for 3 hours or until beans are tender. Remove from heat and press through a sieve. Add the lemon juice and serve.

Mrs. Viola Ammons, Canton, Oklahoma

LIMA BEAN SOUP

2 c. dried lima beans	1 tsp. sugar
1 sm. onion, chopped	1 c. canned tomatoes
1 sm. green pepper, chopped	1 tbsp. flour
2 tsp. salt	2 tbsp. butter

Place the beans in a saucepan and cover with water. Soak overnight. Add enough water to cover. Add the onion and green pepper and cook until beans are tender. Add the salt, sugar and tomatoes and cook for 15 minutes longer. Remove from heat and press through a sieve. Return to saucepan. Mix the flour with a small amount of water and stir into the soup. Bring to a boil and remove from heat. Add butter and serve. 1 quart.

Mildred Wise Howe, Dillwyn, Virginia

FRESH CORN AND CHEESE SOUP

1 c. chopped onions	4 c. corn, cut from cob
1 clove of garlic, chopped	4 c. milk
1 c. diced celery	1/4 tsp. chili powder
1/4 c. butter or margarine	1/4 tsp. pepper
1/4 c. flour	Dash of cayenne pepper
1 1/2 tsp. salt	2 c. shredded American cheese
2 c. hot water	2 tbsp. lemon juice
1/2 c. diced carrots	

Saute the onions, garlic and celery in butter in a kettle for about 10 minutes or until tender. Blend in the flour and salt. Add the water and cook, stirring, until smooth and thickened. Add the carrots and corn and simmer for 15 minutes. Add the milk, seasonings and cheese and heat just until cheese melts. Do not boil. Stir in the lemon juice just before serving. 2 quarts.

Mrs. Agapito G. Saenz, Concepcion, Texas

DILLED SPLIT PEA SOUP

3 strips bacon	1/4 c. finely chopped onion
1 c. split peas	1 tall can evaporated milk
3 c. water	1/2 tsp. dillweed
1 tsp. salt	Dash of cayenne pepper

Fry the bacon in a skillet until crisp, then drain on absorbent paper. Crumble. Reserve 2 tablespoons bacon fat. Wash the peas. Combine the water, salt and peas in a medium saucepan and bring to a boil. Boil for 2 minutes. Remove from heat and let stand for 1 hour. Do not drain. Add reserved bacon fat and onion to peas and cover. Bring to a boil and reduce heat. Simmer for about 40 minutes or until peas are tender. Add undiluted evaporated milk, dillweed and cayenne pepper and heat to serving temperature. Do not boil. Garnish with bacon. Blend the peas and liquid in an electric blender for several seconds or press through a sieve or ricer for a smoother soup. 6 servings.

Photograph for this recipe on page 168.

CURRIED CARROT VICHYSSOISE

1 10 1/4-oz. can frozen cream of potato soup, thawed	1 tsp. curry powder
1 10-oz. package frozen whole baby carrots	2 c. light cream
	Chopped fresh mint

Press the soup through a sieve or whirl in a blender. Cook the carrots according to package directions. Drain and press through a sieve or whirl in a blender. Combine the pureed potato soup, pureed carrots and curry powder in a bowl and stir in the cream gradually. Chill for at least 4 hours. Serve in chilled bowls and garnish with mint. 6 servings.

Curried Carrot Vichyssoise (above)

DELICIOUS BEET SOUP

2 c. sliced cooked beets	Cinnamon to taste (opt.)
2 c. water	3 tbsp. vinegar
2 tbsp. sugar	4 eggs, beaten
Salt and pepper to taste	4 tbsp. sour cream

Combine the beets, water, sugar, salt, pepper and cinnamon in a saucepan and heat to boiling point. Reduce heat and simmer for 10 minutes. Add the vinegar and heat just to boiling point. Mix small amount of beet liquid with eggs, then stir back into the soup. Add the sour cream and serve. May be served cold.

Mrs. Annie Jones, Catawba, North Carolina

CORN AND CHICKEN SOUP

1 c. canned corn	1 c. cream
1/2 c. diced celery	Flour
1 c. diced chicken	1/2 c. milk
4 c. chicken stock	Salt and pepper to taste

Simmer the corn, celery and chicken in stock in a saucepan for 25 minutes. Add the cream. Blend enough flour into milk to thicken soup to desired consistency. Stir into the soup and season with salt and pepper. Cook for 5 minutes.

Mrs. Sally K. Kemp, Columbia, South Carolina

HOME-STYLE TOMATO SOUP

1/2 c. chopped celery	1 tsp. salt
1/4 c. chopped onion	Dash of pepper
1/4 c. chopped green pepper	6 c. milk
1 No. 2 1/2 can tomatoes	

Cook the celery, onion and green pepper in 1 cup boiling, salted water in a saucepan until tender. Add the tomatoes and cook for 7 minutes. Season with salt and pepper. Scald the milk in a double boiler. Stir in the tomato mixture and serve at once. 4-6 servings.

Idella I. Alfson, Savannah, Georgia

PENNSYLVANIA DUTCH POTATO SOUP

2 c. diced potatoes	2 c. milk
1 c. water	1/8 tsp. celery salt
2 tbsp. minced onion (opt.)	Salt and pepper to taste
2 tbsp. margarine or butter	1 hard-cooked egg, chopped
2 tbsp. flour	

Cook the potatoes in water in a saucepan for 15 minutes or until tender. Brown the onion in margarine in another saucepan and blend in flour. Stir in 1/2 cup milk. Add to potatoes, then add the seasonings and remaining milk. Cook, stirring occasionally, until thickened. Garnish with egg. 4 servings.

Mrs. Rose Ann Murphy, Greenville, South Carolina

SCALLOPED CORN CHOWDER

3 tbsp. butter or margarine	1 c. cooked whole kernel corn
1 lge. onion, sliced	2 tsp. salt
5 med. potatoes, diced	Dash of pepper
1 c. scallops	Dash of paprika
2 c. boiling water	1 qt. milk

Melt the butter in a Dutch oven. Add the onion and cook until tender but not brown. Add the potatoes, scallops and water and cover. Simmer for 10 minutes or until potatoes are tender. Add the corn, salt, pepper, paprika and milk and heat through. Garnish with parsley, if desired. 6-8 servings.

Mrs. C. J. Fowler, Jasper, Alabama

HEARTY CORN CHOWDER

1 10 1/4-oz. can frozen cream of potato soup, thawed	1/2 tsp. salt
	1/8 tsp. cracked pepper
1 17-oz. can golden cream-style corn	1 6-oz. package frozen crab meat, thawed
1 c. milk	3 tbsp. snipped fresh parsley

Combine the potato soup, corn, milk, salt and pepper in a medium saucepan and heat to serving temperature, stirring frequently. Add the crab meat and parsley and heat through. 6 servings.

Hearty Corn Chowder (above)

Hearty Mushroom Soup (below)

HEARTY MUSHROOM SOUP

1 env. Swiss hearty beef	**1 env. Swiss cream of**
soup mix	**mushroom soup**
5 c. water	**1 c. milk**

Combine the soup mixes in a large saucepan and stir in water gradually. Bring to a boil, stirring constantly. Reduce heat and cover partially. Simmer for 10 minutes, stirring frequently. Stir in the milk and heat through. 6-8 servings.

PUMPKIN SOUP

1 16-oz. can pumpkin	**1/2 tsp. ginger**
1/2 c. sugar	**1/4 tsp. cloves**
1/2 tsp. salt	**1 2/3 c. evaporated milk**
1 tsp. cinnamon	**2 tbsp. butter**

Combine all ingredients except the butter in top of a double boiler. Place over boiling water and heat through. Stir in the butter. Add more milk if thinner consistency is desired. 4 servings.

Bethany Radtke, Baton Rouge, Louisiana

TOMATO SOUP

4 qt. cooked tomatoes	**1/2 c. sugar**
2 med. onions, chopped	**2 tbsp. cornstarch**
1/4 lb. margarine or butter	**Dash of salt and pepper**

Press tomatoes through a sieve. Brown the onions in butter in a kettle, then press through the sieve. Combine the tomatoes and onions in the kettle. Add the sugar, cornstarch, salt and pepper and bring to a boil. Pour into sterilized jars and seal. Heat to serve. 4-6 pints.

Phyllis White, Nashville, Tennessee

PARMESAN CORN CHOWDER

1 3-in. square salt pork	2 to 3 c. milk
1 c. chopped celery	1 tsp. salt
1 lge. onion, chopped	1/2 tsp. pepper
3 c. chicken broth	1 c. grated Parmesan cheese
2 1-lb. cans cream-style corn	

Dice the salt pork and place in a large kettle. Cook over low heat, stirring, until almost crisp. Add the celery, onion and chicken broth and simmer for about 1 hour or until vegetables are tender. Add the corn and simmer for 30 minutes longer. Add enough milk for desired consistency. Add salt and pepper and heat through. Do not boil. Pour into bowls and sprinkle with cheese. 4-6 servings.

Mrs. J. A. Satterfield, Fort Worth, Texas

FRESH VEGETABLE SOUP

2 ears of corn	1 sm. hot pepper
1/2 c. butter beans	1/2 c. sliced okra
1 qt. tomatoes	1 tbsp. salt
1/4 c. water	1/4 c. vinegar
1 onion, chopped	1/2 c. shortening
1 bell pepper, chopped	1/8 c. sugar

Cut the kernels from corn and place in a saucepan. Add remaining ingredients and cook until vegetables are tender.

Mrs. Lewis A. Jackson, Roopville, Georgia

CREAMY CUCUMBER SOUP

2 lb. peeled cucumbers, chopped	1 green pepper, chopped (opt.)
Salt and pepper to taste	1 tbsp. butter or margarine
1/2 c. hot water	2 c. light cream
1 med. onion, chopped	2 tbsp. chopped parsley
1 clove of garlic, chopped (opt.)	

Combine the cucumbers, salt, pepper, water, onion, garlic and green pepper in a saucepan and cook until vegetables are tender. Remove from heat and cool. Place in blender container and blend. Place back in the saucepan and add butter and cream. Heat through, then sprinkle with parsley. May be served cold. 6 servings.

Isabel Dalmas, Valdese, North Carolina

Calorie-conscious homemakers know that vegetables are a boon — they are low in calories but high in nutritional values. The chart below was prepared to aid you in determining the caloric value of the vegetables you serve every day. Those with particularly low calories have been marked with an asterisk (*).

If weight loss is your goal, consult the herb and spice chart on pages 12 and 13. It will help you replace such high-calorie touches as melted butter or sour cream. There are no calories in seasonings — but they can go a long way toward enhancing the already delicious flavors of every vegetable on your diet!

VEGETABLES
calorie chart

FOOD	PORTION	CALORIES
*Asparagus:		
cut spears, cooked	1 cup	35
spears, canned	six	20
Beans:		
baby lima	1 cup	150
* green	1 cup	25
navy	1 cup	230
red kidney	1 cup	230
* wax or yellow	1 cup	25
*Beet Greens	1 cup	40
Beets	1 cup	70
Broccoli	1 cup	45
Brussels Sprouts	1 cup	60
Cabbage:		
cooked	1 cup	40
* raw, shredded	1 cup	25
Carrots:		
cooked	1 cup	95
* raw	one	20
grated	1 cup	95
Cauliflower:		
cooked	1 cup	30
* raw	1 cup	25
*Celery	1 cup	24

FOOD	PORTION	CALORIES
Collards, cooked	1 cup	75
Corn:		
canned, cream style	1/2 cup	90
canned, whole kernel	1/2 cup	80
cooked	1 ear	65
Cucumber:		
* 6 slices, pared		5
one cucumber, raw, pared		25
Lettuce:		
one head, compact		70
one head, loose leaf		30
* 2 large or 9 small leaves		5
Mushrooms, canned	1 cup	30
Mustard greens, canned	1 cup	30
Okra, cooked	8 pods	30
Onions:		
cooked	1 cup	80
* raw	one 2 1/2" diameter	50
	1 tbsp., chopped	5
young green	six	25
Parsnips	1 cup	95
Peas, green:		
canned	1 cup	170
fresh, cooked	1 cup	110
***Peppers, green**	1 medium	15
Potatoes:		
baked	one	90
boiled	1 cup	105
canned	3-4 small	95
french-fried	10 pieces	100
mashed, milk and butter	1 cup	230
Spinach, cooked	1 cup	45
Squash, cooked:		
summer	1 cup	35
winter	1 cup	95
Sweet Potatoes:		
baked	one	155
boiled	one	170
candied	one	295
canned	1 cup	245
Tomatoes:		
canned or cooked	1 cup	45
* raw	one, medium	30
Turnips, cooked	1 cup	40

Buying vegetables at the height of their growing season is a long-practiced household economy. At such times, they are lowest in price — and at the peak of their fresh flavor goodness.

The following chart was prepared to help you in planning which fresh vegetables you can serve year-round. However, it represents a median — the average months when the vegetables listed are in season. Your proximity to or distance from the growing areas will naturally affect both availability and price. Checking the agricultural listings in your newspaper will help you determine which vegetables are most readily available in your locality and during which months. Watch for supermarket specials, too. They're a guide to what vegetables are in plentiful supply.

buying vegetables
IN SEASON

Month	Vegetables Available (*indicates peak of availability)
January	broccoli*, Brussels sprouts, cabbage, carrots, celeriac, celery, Chinese cabbage*, chives, collards*, endive-escarole*, kale*, leeks*, lettuce-romaine, mushrooms, mustard greens*, onions, parsley, parsnips, peppers, potatoes, shallots, spinach, squash, sweet potatoes, turnips-rutabagas, watercress
February	artichokes, broccoli*, cabbage, carrots, celeriac*, celery, Chinese cabbage, chives, collards, endive-escarole*, kale, leeks, lettuce-romaine, mushrooms, mustard greens, onions, parsley, parsnips, peppers, potatoes, shallots, spinach, squash, sweet potatoes, turnips-rutabagas, watercress
March	artichokes*, asparagus, broccoli, cabbage*, carrots*, celeriac, celery*, Chinese cabbage, chives*, collards, dandelion greens, endive-escarole*, garlic*, kale, leeks*, lettuce-romaine, mushrooms, onions, parsley, parsnips*, peas (green), peppers, potatoes, shallots*, spinach*, squash, sweet potatoes, turnips-rutabagas, watercress*
April	artichokes*, asparagus*, broccoli*, cabbage*, carrots*, celery*, Chinese cabbage, chives, dandelion greens*, escarole-endive, garlic, leeks, lettuce-romaine, onions, parsley, peas (green)*, peppers, potatoes, spinach, squash, sweet potatoes, turnips-rutabagas, watercress*

Month	Vegetables Available (*indicates peak of availability)
May	asparagus*, beans (snap), cabbage*, carrots*, celery*, Chinese cabbage, chives, corn, cucumbers, dandelion greens, endive-escarole, lettuce-romaine, onions*, onions (green), parsley*, peas (green), peppers, potatoes, radishes*, spinach, squash, tomatoes*, turnips-rutabagas, watercress*
June	asparagus, beans (lima), beans (snap)*, beets*, cabbage, carrots, celery, Chinese cabbage, chives, corn, cucumbers*, dandelion greens, endive-escarole, kohlrabi*, lettuce-romaine, okra, onions, onions (green)*, parsley*, peas (green), peppers, potatoes, radishes*, spinach, squash, tomatoes*, turnips-rutabagas, watercress
July	beans (lima)*, beans (snap)*, beets, cabbage, carrots, celery, Chinese cabbage, chives, corn*, cucumbers*, eggplant, endive-escarole, kohlrabi, lettuce-romaine, okra*, onions, onions (green)*, parsley, peppers*, potatoes, radishes, spinach, squash, tomatoes*, turnips-rutabagas, watercress
August	beans (lima)*, beans (snap), beets, cabbage, carrots, celery, Chinese cabbage, chives, corn*, cucumbers, eggplant*, endive-escarole, kohlrabi, lettuce-romaine, okra*, onions, onions (green), parsley, peppers*, potatoes, squash, tomatoes*, turnips-rutabagas, watercress
September	beans (lima), beans (snap), beets, Brussels sprouts, cabbage, carrots, cauliflower, celery, Chinese cabbage, chives, corn, eggplant, endive-escarole, garlic*, kohlrabi, lettuce-romaine, okra, onions, parsley, peppers, potatoes, spinach, squash, tomatoes*, turnips-rutabagas, watercress
October	beans (lima), beans (snap), broccoli, Brussels sprouts*, cabbage, cauliflower*, celery, Chinese cabbage, chives, eggplant, endive-escarole, kohlrabi, lettuce-romaine, okra, onions, parsley, peppers, potatoes, pumpkins*, spinach, squash, sweet potatoes, tomatoes, turnips-rutabagas, watercress
November	broccoli, Brussels sprouts*, carrots, celeriac, celery, Chinese cabbage, chives, endive-escarole, leeks, lettuce-romaine, mushrooms*, onions, parsley*, peppers, potatoes, shallots*, spinach, squash*, sweet potatoes*, turnips-rutabagas*
December	broccoli, Brussels sprouts, cabbage, carrots, celeriac*, celery, Chinese cabbage*, chives*, collards, endive-escarole, kale*, leeks, lettuce-romaine, mushrooms*, mustard greens, onions, parsley, peppers, potatoes, shallots, spinach, squash, sweet potatoes*, turnips

NUTRITION GUIDE

Vegetable	Size Serving Equivalent to 100 Grams	Nutrients per 100 Grams Vitamins	Minerals
Asparagus	6 spears	A, C	
Beans (lima)	2/3 cup	C, B_1	iron
Beans (snap)	3/4 cup	A, C	iron
Beets	2 2 1/4" diam.	C	iron
Beet greens	1/4 lb.	A*, C	iron*
Broccoli	1/4 lb.	A*, C*, B_2	calcium, iron
Brussels sprouts	seven	C*	iron
Cabbage	1/4 lb.	C*	
Carrots	2-4" long	A*	iron
Cauliflower	1/3 small head	C*	
Celery	6 stalks	C	
Collard greens	1/4 lb.	A*, C*, B_1, B_2	calcium*, iron
Corn	1 ear	C, B_1	
Cucumbers	14 slices	C	
Dandelion greens	1/4 lb.	A*, C, B_1	calcium, iron*
Eggplant	1-4" slice		
Endive	1/4 lb.	A*, C	iron
Kale	1/4 lb.	A*, C*, B_2	calcium*, iron
Lettuce (iceberg)	1/3 head	A, C	
Lettuce (leaf)	10 lg. leaves	A, C	iron
Mustard greens	1/4 lb.	A*, C*, B_2	calcium*, iron
Okra	5-10 pods	A, C*	calcium
Onions	2 medium	C	
Parsley	1 bunch	A*, C*	calcium, iron*
Parsnips	1 small	C	
Peas (green)	3/4 cup	A, C*, B_1	
Peppers	1 large	A, C*	
Potatoes	1 small	C	
Pumpkin	1/2 cup	A*, C	
Radishes	10 small	C	iron
Spinach	1/4 lb.	A*, C*, B_2	
Squash (summer)	3/4 cup	C	
Squash (winter)	1/2 cup	A*, C	
Sweet potatoes	2/3 medium	A*, C	
Tomatoes	1 small	A, C	
Turnips	3/4 cup	C	
Turnip greens	1/4 lb.	A*, C*, B_2*	calcium*, iron

*Indicates excellent source of vitamin or mineral.

INDEX

PHOTOGRAPHY CREDITS: United Fresh Fruit and Vegetable Association; Anderson, Clayton & Company: Seven Seas Dressing; American Mushroom Institute; Florida Fruit and Vegetable Association; McIlhenny Company; Florida Citrus Commission; Accent International; American Lamb Council; Ocean Spray Cranberries, Incorporated; Processed Apples Institute; Grandma's West Indies Molasses; Keith Thomas Company; National Dairy Council; Spanish Green Olive Commission; Procter & Gamble Company: Crisco Division; Louisiana Yam Commission; California Artichoke Advisory Board; Brussels Sprouts Marketing Program; General Foods Kitchens; National Meat Canners Association; American Dry Milk Institute; American Dairy Association; Canned Salmon Institute; South African Rock Lobster Service Corporation; Angostura-Wuppermann Corporation; Evaporated Milk Association; Campbell Soup Company; National Association of Frozen Food Packers; Green Giant Company; Best Foods: A Division of Corn Products Company International, Incorporated.

Printed in the United States of America.